大学入試　レベル別英語長文問題
Solution 最新テーマ編2　ハイレベル

別冊問題　もくじ

問題 1

制限時間20分／398 words／解答：本冊p.16

次の英文を読んで、設問 A. 〜 E. に答えよ。

A hundred years ago, less than 2 percent of the population in the United States slept six hours or less a night. Now, (1) almost 30 percent of American adults do. The lens of a 2013 survey by the National Sleep Foundation pulls this sleep deficiency into sharp focus. More than 65 percent of the US adult population fail to obtain the recommended seven to nine hours of sleep each night during the week. Circumnavigate the globe, and (2) things look no better. In the UK and Japan, for example, 39 and 66 percent, respectively, of all adults report sleeping fewer than seven hours. Sleep neglect is common throughout all developed nations, and it is for these reasons that the World Health Organization now labels the lack of societal sleep as a global health epidemic. (3) Taken as a whole, one out of every two adults across all developed countries will not get the necessary sleep they need this coming week.

Importantly, many of these individuals do not report wanting or needing less sleep. If you look at sleep time in the developed nations for the weekends, the numbers are very different. Rather than a mere 30 percent of adults getting eight hours of sleep or more on average, almost 60 percent of these individuals attempt to catch up on eight or more hours of lost sleep. Each weekend, vast numbers of people are desperately trying to pay back a sleep debt they've built up during the week. However, as we have learned time and again, sleep is not like a credit system or the bank. The brain can never recover all the sleep it has been deprived of. (4) We cannot accumulate a debt without penalty, nor can we repay that sleep debt at a later time.

Beyond any single individual, why should society care? Would altering sleep attitudes and increasing sleep amounts (5) (①) any (②) (③) (④) (⑤) as a human race, to our professions and corporations, to commercial productivity, to salaries, the education of our children, or even our moral nature? Whether you are a business leader or employee, the director of a hospital, a practicing doctor or nurse, a government official or military person, a public-policy maker or community health worker, anyone who expects to receive any form of medical care at any moment in their life, or a parent, the answer is very much "yes," for more reasons than you may imagine.

A. 下線部(1)に意味が最も近いものを下のア～エから選び、記号で答えよ。

ア. almost 30 percent of American adults sleep less than most people

イ. close to 30 percent of American adults sleep more than six hours a night

ウ. nearly 30 percent of American adults get six hours or less of sleep a night

エ. only 30 percent of American adults sleep more than people did a hundred years ago

B. 下線部(2)に意味が最も近いものを下のア～エから選び、記号で答えよ。

ア. good things appear

イ. the situations appear similar

ウ. we can look at the world better

エ. we can see objects clearly

C. 下線部(3)を日本語に訳せ。

D. 下線部(4)を日本語に訳せ。

E. 下線部(5)の空所(①)～(⑤)を下のア～オで埋め、本文の内容に最もふさわしい英文を完成させるとき、空所(①)(③)(⑤)に入るものをそれぞれ記号で答えよ。ただし、いずれの記号も1回ずつしか使えない。

ア. collective lives　イ. difference　ウ. make

エ. our　オ. to

問題 2

制限時間25分／491 words／解答：本冊p.26

Read the following text and answer the questions.

Are you familiar with EQ, or "Emotional Intelligence"? Even as of 2004, less than 25 percent of our seminar participants said, yes. This surprised me, since Emotional Intelligence, first popularized by Daniel Goleman in 1995, is a fire that spread well beyond its initial spark among the personal and professional development industries. Let's fan the flames.

What is EQ?

Daniel Goleman defines EQ as "The ability to manage ourselves and our relationships effectively." I think of EQ as "IQ of the heart." But whereas your IQ (intelligence quotient) rarely, if ever, improves with age, you can increase your emotional intelligence from whatever level it is today. And you can increase your staff's emotional intelligence, too.

Why Focus on EQ?

Would you like your staff to (1) <u>adapt</u> more quickly to change and respond better to setbacks and obstacles? Four leading international companies reported that EQ competencies account for (2) <u>approximately</u> 80 percent of job performance. If any one factor figures as much as this, it must at least be worth a look.

EQ, Gender and Culture

If EQ is the ability to manage yourself and your relationships, you can see right away that it cuts across gender and culture. According to research by Professor Cary Cherniss of Rutgers University, 75 percent of top managers in Germany, Latin America and Japan possess high EQ.

You might think that either men or women are "better at EQ," but according to Goleman, each gender tends to demonstrate higher EQ in specific areas; for example, women are on average more aware of their emotions and show more empathy, whereas men are, again on average, more self-confident, (3) <u>optimistic</u> and handle change more easily.

The field is relatively young, scientifically speaking, and more research is being done that has (4) <u>fueled</u> some controversy. After all, measuring "human effectiveness at managing relationships" is bound to cause difficulties. But regardless of what the final word on Emotional Intelligences is, every leader will want to work on the skills that EQ measures, namely self-awareness, emotional self-control and empathy.

Three Ways to Increase Your EQ Today

If you're interested in increasing your EQ, here are three tips:

1. [I]

Effective listening improves every relationship, and you'd be surprised how much better others listen after they've truly been heard.

2. [II]

Beyond the obvious — tears of sadness or joy, for example — see if you can tell what someone is feeling simply by the way they are carrying themselves. Are they bored? Worried? Watch a movie with the sound off for a few minutes and play a game with others called "Spot the Emotion." Professional actors have honed their skills such that you should be able to tell what feelings they're expressing even without hearing their words.

3. [Ⅲ]

(5) Pepper your conversations with sincere, empathetic lines such as, "That must have been (6) tough," or, "You sound like you really enjoyed that." Doing so shows your counterpart that you're interested in both the factual and emotional content of their stories.

Question1 Identify these statements as true or false. Write "T" or "F" on the answer sheet.

(a) EQ can change over time.
(b) Managers often have high emotional intelligence.
(c) Women generally have higher EQ than men.
(d) People have been studying EQ for a long time.
(e) Measuring EQ is easy.

Question2 Choose words with similar meanings to the underlined words (1) to (6). Fill in the box on the answer sheet with the letter (a) - (i). You may use each item only once.

(a) adjust	(b) difficult	(c) generous
(d) modify	(e) positive	(f) roughly
(g) sprinkle	(h) stimulate	(i) strong

Question3 Choose the most appropriate subtitle for each space [Ⅰ] to [Ⅲ].

(a) Reflect others' feelings and achievements with supportive feedback
(b) Improve your relationships with colleagues
(c) Concentrate on specific factual information
(d) Look for emotional clues in body language
(e) Be aware of potential listening blocks
(f) Always tell the truth

問題 3

制限時間20分／455 words／解答:本冊p.42

次の文は“facial recognition technology”について説明した文章です。この内容を踏まえ、問1～問5に答えなさい。

Facial recognition technology uses images captured by digital cameras to identify or confirm an individual's personal identity. (1) It does this by checking the “biometric data”* contained in those camera images against people's facial data (for example, size and shape of face, eye color, etc.) contained in government or commercial databases. Today, it is most commonly used in security systems to check people for access to secure places, computers, or computer networks. In many countries, it is also increasingly used by government agencies — especially by police and other law enforcement or public security agencies — for surveillance** of people's movements and activities in public areas.

Hyogo College of Medicine has introduced a facial recognition technology-based system to check student attendance. It is the first university in Japan to use such a system, according to the institution in the city of Nishinomiya, Hyogo Prefecture. The university expects the system to allow teachers to check students' attendance swiftly and accurately and improve the work efficiency of its staff who, until recently, had been using standard attendance sheets.

Sixteen tablet devices with facial recognition functions were introduced on Friday last week, with four units — one for teachers and three for students — spread across four lecture rooms. The faces of a total of some 470 students had been registered on the devices beforehand. At the start of classes, students register their attendance using the tablets in turn. The devices are held up to their faces, and the images shown on the displays are checked against the preregistered images.

If the facial recognition functions do not work, students enter their identification numbers on the tablets for attendance registration. Teachers can check the attendance on their tablets, which show images of students conducting the facial recognition process in real time. (2) <u>The college also hopes to utilize the new system to identify long-term absentees at an early stage so that appropriate counseling will be provided to them</u>.

The facial recognition system frees teachers from the chore of handing out attendance cards to students and collecting them, as well as entering attendance information into the college's educational affairs system. With the new system, the college expects to cut some 425 hours of such burdensome work in the 1,700 lectures held in a year. In the future, the school plans to use the system for security-related matters. "Previously, it had been difficult for us to watch over our students in a comprehensive manner as no homeroom activities or similar sessions are available at universities," said Keiichiro Suzuki, deputy chief of the college. The system will help increase trust from students and parents in the college and (3) [attendance, nuisance, related, checking, prevent, to] in case classes are formed according to the levels of students' proficiency.

注）*biometric data : 生体データ　　　　**surveillance : 監視

問1 下線部（1）をItとthisの内容を明らかにして、日本語に訳しなさい。

問2 下線部（2）を日本語に訳しなさい。

問3 次の質問に英語で答えなさい。

（1） How many tablets does each classroom use for the new attendance system?

（2） What should students do if the system does not recognize their faces?

問4 文中の（3）［　　　　　］内の語句を正しい順序に並べ替えなさい。

問5 教員の授業運営面からみて、このシステムにはどのようなメリットがあると本文では述べられていますか。日本語で答えなさい。

問題 4

制限時間25分／525 words／解答：本冊p.56

Read the following passage and answer the questions below. (As for the words marked with an asterisk (*), see the notes at the end of the passage.)

Health News

November 1, 2016

Using, and even just thinking about portable media may *disrupt kids' sleep

Children and teens with access to tablets and smartphones at night don't get enough sleep and are sleepier during the day, whether or not they use the devices, according to a new review.

The review of 20 previous studies found kids using portable media devices around bedtime were more than twice as likely as kids who didn't use them to have short sleep times, but so were kids who had access to such devices at night but didn't use them.

"A lot of people argue that it's the device light emission that leads to sleep outcomes, but even if you're not using it, (A) even having the presence of the device near you affects sleep," said lead author Ben Carter of King's College London.

"My personal view is it's due to (a) stimulation from things like social media engagement," and that there may be a similar relationship with adults, Carter told *Reuters Health.

"Your social group is (b) and you can be thinking about it," he said. "If I text a loved one an hour before bed then I'm hoping I might get a reply."

The reviews included studies of children aged 6 to 19 years that measured exposures to portable media like tablets and smartphones, but excluded studies that looked at television, personal computers or sources of electromagnetic *radiation. In total, the included studies covered more than 125,000 children.

Bedtime media device use was consistently linked to difficulty falling asleep or staying asleep and poor daytime function due to sleepiness. Bedtime device use was also tied to (c) sleep times of less than 10 hours per night for children and less than nine hours for teens.

Kids with bedtime access to these devices at least three times a week around bedtime, or with a device in the sleep environment, also had poorer measures of sleep quality and quantity than kids with less or no access.

"It's normal to wake up during the night but when the phone is there, many people instead of just turning over will tap on the phone *ostensibly to check the time, will see 15 text messages from their *buddy or whatever, then 2 hours later they're going back to bed," said Dr. Charles Czeisler at Brigham and Women's Hospital in Boston.

"It's very *engaging technology and when it's present in the bedroom it reduces sleep duration," said Czeisler, who *coauthored an editorial alongside the review.

Two-thirds of teens leave a device (d) while sleeping in bed at night, and turning the device (e) or moving it to another room can make a big difference, he told Reuters Health.

"Device use is *ubiquitous and they are hugely beneficial in some cases," Carter said. "However, we need to recognize that there are negative consequences of some device use."

Some devices can be programmed to switch off at a certain hour, which Carter would strongly encourage, he said.

Poor sleep has been tied to many health outcomes, among them *dementia, Carter said. "Sleep is an exposure that we take for granted, is free and we don't take enough notice of it."

Notes

*disrupt : interrupt

*Reuters : an international news agency

*radiation : heat, energy, etc. that is sent out in the form of rays

*ostensibly : apparently

*buddy : a close friend

*engaging : attractive, fascinating

*coauthor : be a joint author of

*ubiquitous : existing everywhere

*dementia : a serious mental disorder caused by brain disease or injury

1. Translate the underlined part (A) into Japanese.

2. Write the number of the best word to fill in each of the blanks (a) – (c). Do not use the same word more than once.

① active ② continuous ③ insufficient

3. Write the number of the best word to fill in each of the blanks (d) and (e). Do not use the same word more than once.

① against ② for ③ in ④ off ⑤ on

4. Choose two true sentences from the list below.

① All that children and teens should do is to avoid using tablets or smartphones at night if they want to get enough sleep.

② As all devices automatically switch off at a certain hour, children and teens will be protected from the negative consequences.

③ When people wake up during the night and the phone is near the bed, they often read their text messages, which affects their sleep.

④ People tend to overlook the importance of sleep and, as a result, they suffer from health problems.

⑤ Device use is beneficial, so we don't need to worry about its harmful aspects.

5. Translate the underlined part of the following Japanese into English. You can use expressions from the passage.

よく眠るのが難しい人もいる。これには科学技術の発展が関係あるのかもしれない。科学技術は我々の生活をより快適にするはずなのだが。

問題 5

制限時間25分／575 words／解答：本冊p.74

次の英文を読み、設問に答えなさい。

Up to 85 percent of the jobs that today's college students will have in 11 years haven't been invented yet. That's according to a panel of experts assembled by the Institute for the Future, although an exact percentage is impossible to predict. The IFTF, an organization that seeks to identify emerging trends and their impacts on global society, forecasts that many of the tasks and duties of the jobs that today's young people will hold in 2030 don't exist right now.

"Those who plan to work for the next 50 years have to have a mindset of, 'I'm going to be working and learning and working and learning, and working and learning,' in order to make a career," says Rachel Maguire, a research director with IFTF. By 2030, we'll likely be living in a world where artificial assistants help us with almost every task, (1) <u>not unlike the way email tries to finish spelling a word for users today</u>. Maguire says it will be like having an assistant working alongside you, taking on tasks at which the human brain does not excel.

The U.S. Bureau of Labor Statistics says today's students will have eight to 10 jobs by the time they are 38. And they won't necessarily have to take time away from any one of those jobs for training or to gain additional qualifications related to their fields. Instead, they'll partner with machines for on-the-job learning, wearing an augmented reality headset that will give them the information they need in real-time to get the work done. "It eliminates the need for people to leave a job in order to learn a new skill so they can level up and earn more money," Maguire says. "It gives the opportunity for people to be able to learn those kinds of new skills and demonstrate proficiency in-the-moment at the job."

And forget about traditional human resources departments or the challenging task of looking for a job on your own. In the future, (2) the job might come to you. Potential employers will draw from different data sources, including online business profiles and social media streams, to find out about a person and their skills. Maguire says there's already a lot of activity around turning employment into a matchmaking endeavor, using artificial intelligence and deep learning to help the right person and the right job find each other.

In theory, this kind of online job matching could lead to (A) bias and discrimination in hiring practices. However, there are (3) potential pitfalls. "We have to make sure that the people who are building these tools aren't informing these tools with their own biases, whether they're intentional or not," Maguire says. "These systems will only be as good as the data that feeds them."

Which leads Maguire to another point. While she doesn't want to sound melodramatic about emerging technologies, she believes it is critical for the public (4) to get engaged now, rather than sitting back and letting technology happen to them. "What do we want from these new technological capabilities, and how do we make sure we put in place the social policies and systems that will result in what it is we all want?" she says. "I have a deep concern that we're just kind of sitting back and letting technology tell us what jobs we'll have and what jobs we won't have, rather than us figuring out how to apply these technologies to improve our lives."

（注）

mindset：考え方
proficiency：熟練
matchmaking：仲介
discrimination：区別、差別
augmented reality：拡張現実、AR
human resources：人材、人事
bias：先入観、偏見
melodramatic：大げさな

設　問

(1) 下線部 (1) の意味として最も適切なものを、以下の選択肢から１つ選びなさい。

（ア）　現在、書き手が自分で単語のスペルを完成させるのとは違って
（イ）　現在、書き手が自分で単語のスペルを完成させるのと同じように
（ウ）　現在、メールが単語のスペルを完成させてくれるのとは違って
（エ）　現在、メールが単語のスペルを完成させてくれるのと同じように

(2) 下線部 (2) the job might come to you となるのはどうしてか、日本語で説明しなさい。

(3) 空欄（　A　）に入る最も適切な語句を、以下の選択肢から１つ選びなさい。

（ア）　further　　（イ）　less
（ウ）　old-fashioned　　（エ）　personal

(4) 下線部(3)について、求職者と雇用者をつなぐオンラインシステムを作るときにどのような危険の可能性があるか、日本語で説明しなさい。

(5) 下線部(4) to get engaged nowとは具体的にどうすることか、日本語で説明しなさい。

(6) 本文の内容を要約したものとして最も適切なものを、以下の選択肢から１つ選びなさい。

（ア） Artificial intelligence will do all our work for us.
（イ） We will all look for jobs online.
（ウ） Our way of working will change significantly in the near future.
（エ） We will assist technology in doing our work.

問題 6

制限時間25分／561 words／解答：本冊p.88

次の英文を読み、設問に答えなさい。

The promise of self-driving cars can be attractive. Imagine taking a nap or watching a movie in a comfortable armchair while being shuttled safely home after a long day at work. But (a) many over-optimistic images of the future, it is a bit of an illusion.

Automated cars may indeed make commuting more pleasurable while preventing accidents and saving many lives — someday. But (b) <u>a recent fatal crash</u> suggests that some of these cars are not ready for the busy American roads: a lot of sensors and software turned this car into a high-tech vehicle you might see in a science fiction movie. In fact, (c) <u>the technology that powers these vehicles could introduce new risks that few people appreciate</u>. For example, when a computer controlling the car does not hit the brakes to avoid a car crash, the person in the driver's seat — many automated cars on the road today still require someone to be there in case of an emergency — may also fail to intervene because the driver trusts the car too much to pay close attention to the road. That is what appears to have happened in the crash.

"Technology does not eliminate error, but it (d) the nature of errors that are made, and it (e) new kinds of errors," said Chesley Sullenberger, the former US Airways pilot who landed a plane in the Hudson River in 2009 after its engines were struck by birds. He now sits on a Department of Transportation advisory committee on automation. "We have to realize that it's not a solution for everything."

What concerns him and other safety experts is that industry executives and government officials are rushing to put self-driving cars on the road without appropriate safeguards and under the (f) that the technology will reduce crashes and fatalities.

Even as officials (g) place a big bet that autonomous cars will solve many of our safety problems, American roads are becoming less safe. More than 37,000 people were killed in 2016, up 5.6 percent from 2015. The death toll is estimated to be more than 40,000 in 2017.

Experts who are skeptical about the unstoppable march of technology say fatalities are rising because public officials have become so fond of the shiny new thing that they have taken their eyes off problems they could be solving today. In the federal government and most states, there appears to be little interest in making policies with proven track records of saving lives now, (h) as opposed to some time in the distant future.

Other industrialized countries have made great progress in reducing traffic crashes over the last two decades. Road fatality rates in Canada, France, Germany and Sweden, for example, are now less than half the rate in the United States. And no, these countries don't have loads of self-driving cars. (i) They have reduced accidents in the old-fashioned way. Some of them have worked to slow down traffic; speed is a leading killer. They have made changes to roads so pedestrians will not have to pay much attention to cars.

European regulators have encouraged the use of seatbelts by putting visual reminders even in the back seat. Germany requires much more rigorous driver education and testing than most American states do.

Mr. Sullenberger is worried that the rush to develop automated cars will lead to many unforeseen problems. "Even though there is a sense of urgency to prevent human-caused accidents, (j)."

(1) 空所（ a ）に入れるのに最も適切な語を次の1～4の中から1つ選びなさい。

1 as　2 like　3 unlike　4 without

(2) 下線部(b)の事故についてこれまでに判明したことは何か。最も適切なものを次の1～4の中から1つ選びなさい。

1 人が乗っていない自動運転車両が起こした。
2 道路を見ていなかった運転手に責任がある。
3 コンピュータの誤作動によって引き起こされた。
4 その原因はまだ特定するまでには至っていない。

(3) 下線部(c)の意味に最も近いものを次の1～4の中から1つ選びなさい。

1 Few people express concerns about dangers introduced by the technology behind self-driving cars.
2 Few people apprehend the new technology used in these modern, powerful vehicles.
3 The technology used in these new cars may cause accidents that are difficult to predict.
4 The technology applied to these modern cars is so powerful that they are unappreciated.

(4) 空所（ d ）と（ e ）に入れるのに最も適切なものの組み合わせを次の1～4の中から1つ選びなさい。

1 (d) introduces (e) introduces
2 (d) introduces (e) changes
3 (d) changes (e) changes
4 (d) changes (e) introduces

(5) 空所（ f ）に入れるのに最も適切なものを次の1～4の中から1つ選びなさい。

1 established theory
2 concealed assumption
3 unproven hypothesis
4 misguided circumstances

(6) 下線部(g)の意味に最も近いものを次の1～4の中から1つ選びなさい。

1 are confident
2 are suspicious
3 do realize
4 do not understand

(7) 下線部(h)の書き換えとして最も適切なものを次の1～4の中から1つ選びなさい。

1 although federal and state lawmakers have spent time preparing bills to save lives in the future
2 because experts have warned that there will be more serious concerns about future risks
3 when public officials should oppose an increase in the future death rate
4 but they nevertheless expect a bright future with no fatal accidents

(8) 下線部(i)にあるようなこととして、その直後の部分で実例が４つ挙げられているが、実はこのうち１つは例としてふさわしくないものに書き換えられている。それはどれか。次の１～４の中から１つ選びなさい。

1 Some of them have worked to slow down traffic.

2 They have made changes to roads so pedestrians will not have to pay much attention to cars.

3 European regulators have encouraged the use of seatbelts by putting visual reminders even in the back seat.

4 Germany requires much more rigorous driver education and testing than most American states do.

(9) 空所（ j ）に入れるのに最も適切なものを次の１～４の中から１つ選びなさい。

1 the government is not working fast enough to fix these problems, nor is the industry

2 the auto industry needs to make money, not in the future but now

3 self-driving cars should neither be banned, nor regulated, because of it

4 we need to do it in a responsible way, not the fastest way

(10) この記事のタイトルとして最も適切なものを次の１～４の中から１つ選びなさい。

1 Time for Automated Vehicles? Think First

2 Making American Roads Safe Again

3 The Potential and Promise of Self-driving Cars

4 Old Versus New Ways of Traffic Control

問題 7

制限時間25分／558 words／解答：本冊p.106

次の英文を読んで下の問いに答えなさい。

Generally speaking, Japanese people do not really like to get wet when it rains. Many people buy new umbrellas when it suddenly rains. As is often the case with the newly bought ones, they end up being left in various places. While 120 to 130 million umbrellas are sold per year in Japan, approximately 80 million plastic ones are (ア)<u>discarded</u> annually, according to the Japan Umbrella Promotion Association and other sources.

A start-up company has successfully launched an umbrella-sharing service, mainly in Tokyo, using "Internet of Things" (IoT) technology to reduce umbrella waste. The company started the service in December 2018, and it aims for the use of all rented umbrellas. The service is called (イ)<u>iKasa</u> since "Kasa" is Japanese for umbrella.

Users of the service register with the company via the LINE messaging app and check for the umbrella spots closest to their location. The user goes to the stand, unlocks their umbrella of choice by scanning the QR code on its handle and checks it out for as long as they need. The service is available for 70 yen per day, paid via a registered credit card.

(ウ)<u>The iKasa system has achieved a 100 percent return rate of rented umbrellas</u>, since the registration of credit card numbers connects the umbrellas to the personal information of users. The

Tokyo-based company has installed iKasa spots at 100 stores, offices and other places that have formed partnerships with it.

(エ) A range of organizations have previously failed in umbrella-sharing programs due to low return rates. For example, the Hakodate Chamber of Commerce and Industry and other organizations in Hakodate, Hokkaido, made 2,300 umbrellas available for free use by tourists, when the Hokkaido Shinkansen line started in March 2016. The tourism promotion program ended a year later because (オ) [1] [2] [3] [4] [5] [6]. A similar program was introduced by the Shibuya Ward in Tokyo about ten years ago, but it failed to last for the same reason.

The iKasa service has overcome the problem of people not returning because it addresses the issue as "a business." The founder of the company said, "We hope to operate across Japan as an (カ) infrastructure such as Japan's excellent railway network."

Other companies are also addressing the waste of umbrellas. A soft drink maker based in the city of Osaka places free-use umbrellas next to its vending machines, mainly in office buildings and shopping streets, because many people notice them and often return to such locations. Umbrellas used by this service include those provided by railways which were left behind on trains and in stations. The corporation started the service in Osaka in 2015 and has since expanded it to Tokyo and 15 prefectures.

In a related development, another company plans to shortly begin a sharing program at Tokyo-area train stations on a trial basis, using umbrellas made of Limex, an innovative material it developed from limestone. The Tokyo-based venture company said it developed the new material [キ] global trends toward reducing plastic use for environmental protection.

As umbrella users, we need to consider not only convenience, but also (ク) how to reduce waste in our societies. That way, we can comfortably stay dry on a rainy day without hurting our environment.

問1 下線部（ア）discardedと最も意味が近いものを、次のa ～ eから1つ選びなさい。

a. abandoned　b. cancelled　c. ceased
d. discharged　e. replaced

問2 下線部（イ）iKasaの説明として最も適切なものを、次のa ～ eから1つ選びなさい。

a. The users are tourists who want to keep umbrellas as souvenirs.
b. The users need QR code readers on the handle of their smartphones.
c. The users can rent umbrellas in town through the Internet.
d. The users can check the type of umbrellas at their closest spots.
e. The users can use the service for free after they have registered their credit cards.

問3 下線部（ウ）<u>The iKasa system has achieved a 100 percent return rate of rented umbrellas</u>の理由を最も適切に述べているものを、次のa ～ eから１つ選びなさい。

a. The iKasa company keeps checking the locations of their umbrellas through the Internet.
b. The iKasa system requires the users to return the umbrellas to the spots located in 15 prefectures.
c. The service identifies the users through the credit card information that they registered.
d. The service requires the users to register their credit cards just in case they forget to pay in cash.
e. The users register how many days they will rent umbrellas beforehand and pay 70 yen a day.

問4 下線部（エ）<u>A range of organizations</u>が行った具体例として最も適切なものを、次のa ～ eから１つ選びなさい。

a. The Japan Umbrella Promotion Association miscounted the number of umbrellas for sharing in Japan.
b. The Hakodate Chamber of Commerce and Industry tried to help tourists by providing an umbrella-sharing program.
c. The stations on the Hokkaido Shinkansen line made 2,300 umbrellas for sale to make more profit.
d. The Shibuya Ward in Tokyo had tourists borrow its umbrellas from 2016 but they ran out of available umbrellas.
e. A drink maker in Osaka placed free-use umbrellas beside its vending machines but users rarely returned to the same location.

問5 下線部（オ）が意味の通る文となるように［ 1 ］～［ 6 ］に以下の語を当てはめ、その記号を解答欄にマークしなさい。ただし、それぞれの語は1度のみ使うものとし、１つ使わない語も含まれている。

a. returned　b. most　c. been　d. few
e. had　f. of　g. the umbrellas

1 ______ 2 ______ 3 ______ 4 ______ 5 ______ 6 ______

1 健康　2 心理　3 IT・テクノロジー　4 健康　5 IT・テクノロジー　6 IT・テクノロジー　7 環境　8 文化　9 環境　10 社会

問6 下線部（カ）infrastructureの説明として最も適切なものを次のa～eの中から１つ選びなさい。

a. a business which has changed into a useful service
b. a framework supporting the scheduling of railways
c. a group of people regarded as supporting an organization
d. the natural or prepared ground on which buildings rest
e. the basic systems and services needed for a society to function

問7 空欄 [キ] に入る最も適切なものを次のa～eから１つ選びなさい。

a. at the mercy of
b. in contrast to
c. in opposition to
d. in line with
e. on the verge of

問8 下線部（ク）how to reduce wasteについて本文の内容に合った行動として最も適切なものを次のa～eの中から１つ選びなさい。

a. buying drinks from vending machines when you return umbrellas
b. choosing the free-use umbrella spot which is closest to your home
c. returning rental umbrellas as quickly as possible to get a refund
d. collecting and throwing away forgotten umbrellas on trains and in stations
e. using a rental umbrella service and always returning your umbrella

問9 本文の内容に最も合うものを次のa～gから2つ選びなさい。

a. The majority of Japanese people rent shared umbrellas when it suddenly rains.
b. About 80 million plastic umbrellas are purchased every year in Japan.
c. A start-up company uses Internet of Things technology to reduce umbrella waste.
d. A railway company in Hokkaido has formed a partnership with the iKasa service in Tokyo.
e. Umbrellas used by the iKasa service include those provided by railways which were left behind on buses and in office buildings.
f. A venture company will soon use umbrellas made of a newly developed material to protect the environment.
g. Limex is a credit card company which gives umbrellas to new customers.

問題 8

制限時間25分／583 words／解答：本冊p.122

次の英文を読み、下の問いに答えなさい。

When Target, a giant discount chain in the US, announced that its stores would stop using signs that directed boys to buy certain toys (such as trucks and toy soldiers) and girls to buy others (such as dolls and pretty costumes), hundreds visited its website to complain. "(1)This is beyond stupid," wrote one customer, promising never to shop at Target. "Boys will always be boys and girls will always be girls!" said another.

But (2)those voices met a great deal of resistance. Many parents and commenters expressed support after the announcement, no doubt because they've started to realize something psychologists have been saying for years: that children will be happier if they're not forced into (3)boxes according to their sexes. It's natural for kids to experiment with different toys and identities. Dismissing such tendencies "can limit how kids view themselves, what skills they develop, and what their interests become," says Debbie Sterling, founder of Goldie Blox, which makes construction toys for girls.

It's also an urge driven in large part by marketing. "There are (X) between males and females," says Stephanie Coontz, an author and historian. In the early 20th century, for example, pink — now a color closely associated with girls — was considered a color more appropriate for boys. During World War II, Coontz notes, women proved that they could do jobs traditionally done by males, like working in factories, while their kids played with toys designed for both girls and boys.

But by the 1980s, toy companies like Mattel and Hasbro had figured out that they could make more money by creating two separate toy markets. And so the era of "blue for boys, pink for girls" (4) exploded; along with it came many new stereotypes about what we should like and how we should be.

These expectations continue well beyond childhood. Today's women, who grew up at a time when girls were not encouraged to pick up toy soldiers, are still excluded from roughly 177,000 posts in the Army, a branch of the military that separated sexes until nearly 1980. Today's men, many of whom were raised to play with toy soldiers rather than baby dolls, still (Y) pursue careers in nursing or child care.

Of course, none of this means that there are no differences between men and women or that emphasizing them can't be helpful. For instance, fighting for equality often means highlighting gaps between the sexes, especially in areas like economic status. "But (5) play is a way to learn about who we become as adults," says Ellen Dubois, who teaches history and gender* at an American university. "Toys and what they signify, which is the free expression of play among children, should be as open and diverse as possible."

Beyond Target's decision, there are signs that we, as a society, are starting to accept more flexible gender roles. Recently, organizers in Utah launched what's believed to be the first all-girls tackle-football* league, and advocates are pushing for more mixed-sex sports for pre-teenage children. "(6) It's healthy for boys to understand that girls can play just as skillfully and with just as much strength as the boys do," says Nancy Hogshead-Makar, a former Olympic swimmer. Not long ago, Seattle became the third city to make it a rule that all single-stall bathrooms* be labeled unisex. The move was driven by people who often say they feel unwelcome in the men's room and the women's room — and who, as kids, were likely to feel as if they were forced into the wrong toy section.

Notes :
gender 社会的・文化的な性差
tackle-football 実際に選手同士が身体をぶつけ合う本格的なアメリカンフットボール
single-stall bathrooms 独立型の公共トイレ

A. 下線部(1)の意味に最も近いものを次の(イ)～(ニ)の中から1つ選びなさい。

(イ) This is almost stupid.
(ロ) This is extremely stupid.
(ハ) This is far from stupid.
(ニ) This is not stupid.

B. 下線部(2)の意味に最も近いものを次の(イ)～(ニ)の中から1つ選びなさい。

(イ) A lot of people having those opinions got together to resist the criticism.
(ロ) A lot of people having those opinions got together to support them.
(ハ) Those opinions were opposed by a lot of people.
(ニ) Those opinions were supported by a lot of people.

C. 下線部(3)とほぼ同じ意味で使われている1語をBut by the 1980s...で始まる第4段落から選び、書きなさい。

D. 空所（ X ）に入る語句として最も適切なものを次の（イ）～（ニ）の中から１つ選びなさい。

（イ） differences but few similarities
（ロ） more differences than similarities
（ハ） more similarities than differences
（ニ） no similarities but only differences

E. 下線部(4)の意味に最も近いものを次の（イ）～（ニ）の中から１つ選びなさい。

（イ） ended once and for all
（ロ） quickly became popular
（ハ） was a complete disaster
（ニ） was suddenly rejected

F. 空所（ Y ）に入る語として最も適切なものを次の（イ）～（ニ）の中から１つ選びなさい。

（イ） rarely　　（ロ） sometimes
（ハ） thoughtfully　　（ニ） willingly

G. 下線部(5)の意味に最も近いものを次の（イ）～（ニ）の中から１つ選びなさい。

（イ） As we become adults, play gives way to work.
（ロ） Play can distract adults from what is really important for them.
（ハ） Play can help us know what we will be like when we become adults.
（ニ） When we become adults, we can still learn something valuable through play.

H. 下線部(6)を句読点も含め50字以内の日本語に訳しなさい。

I. 本文の内容と一致するものを(イ)~(ト)の中から2つ選びなさい。ただし、3つ以上マークした場合は得点を認めません。

(イ) Target has never used signs that directed boys and girls to different sections.

(ロ) Kids have a natural tendency to try different toys to see where their interests lie.

(ハ) Pink, which is now regarded as a color specially for girls, was once believed to be unlucky for boys.

(ニ) Now women can be appointed to any post in the Army so long as they meet certain standards.

(ホ) In order to overcome sexual inequality, it is often necessary to emphasize gaps between males and females.

(ヘ) Almost all the states in the US now have all-girls tackle-football leagues.

(ト) You cannot see unisex single-stall bathrooms in any city other than Seattle now.

問題
9

制限時間30分／514 words／解答：本冊p.138

次の英文A～Eは全体でひとつづきになっています。これを読んで次の(1)～(13)の問いに答えなさい。それぞれの問いに対して、答えをイ～ニの中から１つ選び、その記号を解答欄にマークしなさい。

A　Climate change is greatly affecting our world. It is contributing to an increase in extreme weather, more competition for resources such as water, and a greater number of disease-carrying insects, while at the same time having a negative effect on a wide variety of animals. These animals range from sea turtles to pandas to polar bears. Struggling to survive as Arctic ice melts due to global warming, the polar bear in particular has become a powerful symbol of the (　a　) of climate change. However, there is another, often ignored indicator of the health of our planet: its soundscape.

B　Soundscape ecology is the study of nature's sounds. Using a microphone and a recorder, American soundscape ecologist Bernie Krause has been recording the sounds of California's forests for many years: the gurgle of rivers and the melody of birdsong, the humming of insects. In the nearly 50 years Krause has been doing this, he has created a valuable ①<u>resource</u> for other ecologists to study. He believes strongly in the importance of recording soundscapes, saying, "Natural soundscapes give us information necessary to our (　b　) the natural world. They allow us to perceive whether or not an environment is healthy."

C　Krause's early recordings in the California forests were rich and full of life, a celebration of biodiversity. But when he returned last spring to his usual recording spot in Sugarloaf Ridge Stat. Park, what he heard was shocking. “The sounds of the forest had changed ②significantly,” Krause says. “It was the first spring in my 77 years that I heard no birdsong at all.” This was not entirely unexpected, he explains. California’s forests have been severely affected by years of drought, or lack of rain, due to climate change. As the once-healthy forest habitat is damaged, the animals that live there are falling silent.

D Sadly, Krause has found similar changes in the soundscape of natural habitats around the world from the Amazon to Zimbabwe to Borneo. The (c) of these soundscapes is an urgent warning about the effects of climate change. Krause says the changing soundscapes “③speak strongly to all the climate issues we are now facing, from global warming to shifts in the number and variety of bird, frog and mammal populations.” More than 50 percent of the thousands of unique habitats captured in his recordings are now almost completely silent, unrecognizable because of the damage that humankind has done to the environment.

E Krause says of his earlier recordings, “These are soundscapes that no one will hear again in their natural state. They exist today only as a kind of memory, a digital impression of what once existed.” It is highly likely that Krause’s recordings contain sounds made by undiscovered animals that have now disappeared and will never be known to us. Scientists estimate that in the next 25-30 years, up to one-quarter of the world's species may disappear, ④driven to extinction by climate change. That number could (d) an astonishing 50 percent by 2100. As Krause puts it, “A great silence is spreading over the natural world, at the same time that the sound of humankind is becoming deafening.”

(1) Aの空欄(a)に入るもっとも適切なものを選びなさい。

イ. end　ロ. history　ハ. impact　ニ. uses

(2) Aの内容に合っていないものを選びなさい。

イ. Climate change is leading to a variety of problems globally.

ロ. Illnesses can be spread more widely because of climate change.

ハ. Insects are negatively affecting resources like water.

ニ. The effects of climate change can not only be seen but heard.

(3) Bの下線部①“resource”の意味にもっとも近いものを選びなさい。

イ. assortment of ideas　ロ. collection of data

ハ. group of answers　ニ. variety of arguments

(4) Bの空欄(b)に入るもっとも適切なものを選びなさい。

イ. confidence in　ロ. requirements for

ハ. understanding of　ニ. worries about

(5) Bの内容にもっとも合っているものを選びなさい。

イ. In order to record soundscapes, Krause needs many pieces of equipment.

ロ. It took Krause almost 50 years to discover soundscape ecology.

ハ. Krause believes soundscapes reveal the condition of an environment.

ニ. Krause focuses on the sounds made by trees in the forests of California.

(6) Cの下線部②"significantly"の意味にもっとも近いものを選びなさい。

イ. finally　　ロ. remarkably

ハ. repeatedly　　ニ. silently

(7) Cの内容に合うように、もっとも適切なものを選び、次の英文を完成させなさい。

The lack of birdsong Krause noticed when he returned to his usual recording spot (　　).

イ. made the environment diverse

ロ. occurred since there is less rain in spring

ハ. resulted in climate change

ニ. was shocking but not really surprising to him

(8) Dの空欄(c)に入るもっとも適切なものを選びなさい。

イ. decreasing value　　ロ. growing silence

ハ. improved quality　　ニ. smaller quantity

(9) Dの下線部③"speak strongly to"の意味にもっとも近いものを選びなさい。

イ. are a clear sign of

ロ. are an argument against

ハ. surely provide answers to

ニ. undoubtedly try to predict

(10) Dの内容にもっとも合っているものを選びなさい。

イ. Krause's soundscape recordings have hurt natural habitats everywhere.

ロ. More and more animals are contributing to nature's soundscapes.

ハ. The changing soundscapes tell us the environment is in grave danger.

ニ. The new silence in nature reflects the uniqueness of the planet.

(11) Eの下線部④"driven"の意味にもっとも近いものを選びなさい。

イ. adapted　　ロ. permitted

ハ. pushed　　ニ. related

(12) Eの空欄(d)に入るもっとも適切なものを選びなさい。

イ. compare to　　ロ. fall from

ハ. remain at　　ニ. rise to

(13) Eの内容にもっとも合っているものを選びなさい。

イ. Krause's recordings may be the only proof some species ever existed.

ロ. Quieter soundscapes have led to rapid species loss globally.

ハ. Soundscape ecologists help us protect undiscovered animals.

ニ. Soundscapes are becoming silent in spite of humankind's activities.

問題 10

制限時間25分／582 words／解答：本冊p.154

次の文章を読んで、以下の問いに答えなさい。

"No man is an island, entire of itself; every man is a piece of the continent, a part of the main," wrote the poet John Donne in the 17th Century.

Some people seek isolation, but (ア) <u>few choose to be lonely.</u> Loneliness not only makes us unhappy, but it is bad for us. It can lead to a lack of confidence and mental health problems like depression, stress and anxiety. A report by the Mental Health Foundation suggests loneliness among young people is increasing; at the same time, social changes such as the rise of the solo dweller, combined with an aging population, are changing the way people interact with each other.

So is modern life making us lonely? People feel lonely for different reasons, says Michelle Mitcell, charity director general of Age UK*, but it tends to be triggered by a big life event. "It can be poor health, illness, money, children moving away, feeling cut off from family or community, a lack of access to transport, redundancy* or career problems or divorce. Often it's (イ) <u>when people lose a sense of purpose and contribution.</u>"

"Bereavement* is also a big issue — losing your husband or wife can have a really detrimental* impact on how people feel about the world," Mitchell says. It is a feeling that Pam, whose husband died four years ago, identifies with. "You meet other men, who are on their own. That's not what I am looking for. What am I looking for? I'm looking for my husband, aren't I, and I'm never going to find him," she says.

But while bereavement may be inevitable, there's a sense modern society is exacerbating* other triggers of loneliness. Dr. Andrew McCulloch, chief executive of the Mental Health Foundation, argues that although there is no hard historic data to show loneliness — which is arguably subjective — getting worse, there is some sociological evidence. "We have data that suggests people's social networks have got smaller and families are not providing the same level of social context they may have done 50 years ago. It's not because they are bad or uncaring families, but it's to do with geographical distance, marriage breakdown, (ウ) multiple caring responsibilities and longer working hours," he says.

But if modern society is making us lonelier, what can be done to counter it? Mitchell says there needs to be more investment in social help such as befriending schemes — which relies on volunteers — and community outreach* programs, as being part of a social network such as a walking club or local church can help alleviate* loneliness. She says we also have a responsibility to "think more openly and creatively about how to deal with (エ) one of the greatest social problems of our time".

McCulloch agrees innovation* is key. "Instead of living alone, people could club together to buy houses — a friend is doing that in his old age, it's a mini commercial enterprise," he says. But he says

(オ) there needs to be a cultural shift so that people are more concerned about the welfare of those in their communities. “Just a basic level of social behavior, such as saying hello, or asking if people are OK, can have an impact,” he says.

Mitchell believes a tipping point* is around the corner. “I think we’ll look back and think ‘how did we allow that to happen?’ It’s like looking back at the issue of children going to work at 12 years of age — there’s something so fundamentally wrong with what’s happening,” she says.

注

charity director general of Age UK : Age UK（高齢者のための慈善団体名）の会長
redundancy : 余剰人員の解雇、「リストラ」
bereavement : （親しい者に）先立たれること　　detrimental : 有害な
exacerbate : 悪化させる　　outreach : 福祉を広めるための
alleviate : 軽減する　　innovation : 一新すること
tipping point : 小さな積み重ねがある時点から大きな流れとなる、その転換点

(問1) 下線部（ア）（イ）（ウ）の内容に最も近いものをそれぞれ１つ選びなさい。

（ア）few choose to be lonely

1. it is hard to get rid of noisy neighbors
2. lots of people are forced to live close together
3. no one can tell where loneliness comes from
4. there are not many who prefer loneliness

（イ）when people lose a sense of purpose and contribution

1. when one does not know what to do for oneself or for others
2. when society is disturbed by natural disasters
3. when there is a deep mistrust of government among people
4. when you come to think of your own future

（ウ）multiple caring responsibilities

1. responsibilities to decide whether or not to give aged patients prolonged medical treatment
2. responsibilities to earn a living as well as take care of the housework
3. responsibilities to look after more than one person at the same time
4. responsibilities to take account of various conditions of local residents

(問2) 下線部（エ）の内容を表す１語を本文から抜き出しなさい。

(問3) 下線部（オ）を以下のように言い換えるとき、空欄に入れるのに最も適切なものを１つ選びなさい。

（オ）there needs to be a cultural shift so that people are more concerned about the welfare of those in their communities

↓

there needs to be a cultural shift which will (　　)

1. allow people to live more independently from each other in an ever wealthier society
2. encourage people to think more about their neighbors' health, safety and happiness
3. make people raise more money to support the sick and the aged
4. remind people of the importance of the politeness and diligence of the old days

(問4) 以下の（A）～（C）について、本文の内容に最も近いものをそれぞれ１つ選びなさい。

（A） 1. The aging population has given rise to a generation with enough skills to live independently.
2. The number of people living alone is increasing in the city, but not in the suburban areas.
3. The report by the Mental Health Foundation says loneliness among young people causes changes in the way people interact with each other.
4. What John Donne means is that none of us can live totally isolated from the rest of the world.

（B） 1. Mitchell holds Pam as a fine example of a person overcoming loneliness caused by bereavement.
2. Pam cannot have the same view of the world as she had before her husband died four years ago.
3. Pam is eagerly looking for a future husband, but there are so many candidates that she just cannot choose one.
4. Pam is tired of taking care of her husband and hopes someday he will be able to look after himself.

（C） 1. According to McCulloch, people today are less affectionate towards their family members than they were 50 years ago.
2. McCulloch argues that we need more investment in order to promote various commercial enterprises.
3. McCulloch doubts that small deeds such as saying hello to neighbors have any meaning in our modern society.
4. McCulloch insists on the importance of innovating today's social networks so that people can get closer.

大学入試

レベル別

英語長文問題 Solution

ソリューション

最新テーマ編

2

ハイレベル

スタディサプリ
英語講師
肘井 学
Gaku Hijii

かんき出版

はじめに

“新時代の英語長文集を作ること”。このテーマで『大学入試レベル別英語長文問題ソリューション1 ～ 3』を執筆させていただきました。**「解いて終わり」の英語長文はもう終わり**にして、**「出てきた単語を必ず覚える、そして音読を10回することで、1文1文を自分のものにして先に進む」というコンセプト**は、たくさんの賛同をいただき、多くの教育者の方々に推奨していただけるほどになりました。

本書は、前作の**「音読がしやすい語数」**という最大の特長を維持しつつ、その語数を音読可能な500語台にまで広げて、**最新のテーマを扱う**という趣旨の英語長文問題集です。**食品廃棄問題、AI、自動運転車、海洋汚染、菜食主義、プラスチックごみ、遠隔教育など、最新のトレンドを扱っています。**これらの分野から本番の試験問題が出題される可能性は非常に高いと言っても差し支えないでしょう。

もっとも、入試本番で、本書で扱ったものと同じテーマや同じ文章が出ても、決して油断しないようにしてください。知っている題材や読み込んだ文章が試験に出題されることは大きなアドバンテージになりますが、あくまで**試験当日に見た文章から、客観的に情報を読み取り、その情報から答えを推論すること**、これだけは忘れないでください。

長文中に出てきた単語を必ず覚えること、そして**音読を10回すること**は、**魔法のような相乗効果**をもたらしてくれます。さあ、さっそく本書で音読のパワーを最大限に味わってください！　**皆さんが信じるべきは、毎日の己の地道な努力であること**を、お忘れないように。

肘井　学

目　次

BACKGROUND KNOWLEDGE

本シリーズの特長

特長その❶　4種類のポイントで万全の英語力が身に付く！

本書では、一文一文の理解に役立つ 構文 POINT 、文と文のつながりを見抜く 論理 POINT 、問題の解き方がわかる 解法 POINT 、語彙（ごい）の本質に強くなる 語彙 POINT と、4種類の**POINT**で体系化してあらゆる角度から英語力を向上させていきます（p.8〜p.9参照）。

特長その❷　文構造がひと目でわかる構文図解付き！

構文図解で、SVOCMの記号を使って、解釈の手助けをします。必要に応じて、▲マークで**細かい文法事項のメモを入れており**、**独学でも疑問を残しません**。これと全訳を照らし合わせて、問題を解き終わった後に、**一文一文丁寧に構文把握**をします。

特長その❸　音読用白文・リスニング強化の音声ダウンロード付き！

音読用の白文を掲載しています。**音声ダウンロード**を利用して、音声の後に英文の音読を続けて、**リスニング強化・正確な発音習得**にも役立ててください。問題を解く ⇒ 解説を読む ⇒ 構文把握する ⇒ 単語を覚えた後の**音読10回を必ず行ってください**。

特長その❹　単語帳代わりになる語彙リスト付き！

本書では、本文訳の下に**語彙リスト**を掲載しています。必ず、**出てきた単語をその場で覚えて**ください。

特長その❺　背景知識が広がるコラム付き！

すべての英文に、背景知識が広がるコラムを設けました。背景知識としてあると、**英文を読むのが非常に楽になる**ものを、コラムで紹介しています。自由英作文にはもちろん、他科目にも有効な一生モノの知識が詰まっています。

特長その❻ 最新のテーマを厳選！

時代を反映した最新の頻出テーマである「**食品廃棄問題**」・「**人工知能**」・「**海洋汚染**」・「**菜食主義**」・「**プラスチックごみ問題**」・「**孤独問題**」など、長文の題材を厳選しました。将来の教養として、興味深い題材がそろっています。

特長その❼ 国公立・私立と文系・理系のバランスのとれた題材！

志望大学に左右されない確かな英語力を養うために、出典を**国公立大学と私立大学からバランスよく**選びました。同時に、**文系と理系の両方に精通できる**ような内容を、バランスよく配置しています。

特長その❽ マーク式・記述式の豊富な問題形式・良問揃いの構成！

どの形式でも対応できる英語力を付けるために、**マーク式と記述式の問題をバランスよく配置**しました。さらに、実際の入試問題から、**悪問や奇問を外して、良問をそろえました**。

特長その❾ 音読が可能な300語～500語前後の英文を厳選！

本書で推奨する**音読10回**をやり遂げるために、**音読が可能な300語～500語前後の英文をそろえました**。前作で好評を博した300語前後の文章に加えて、500語前後の文章も扱うことで、より幅広いテーマの英文を扱うことを可能にしました。

4種類のPOINT

構文 POINT

論理 POINT

解法 POINT

語彙 POINT

本シリーズの使い方

❶ 問題を解く

各問題には、制限時間を設けています。それを参考に、**1題20分～30分程度**で、本番を想定して問題を解きます。

⬇

❷ 解答・解説を見て答え合わせをする

悪問・奇問の類は外しています。**4種類のポイント**を中心に解説を読み進めてください。**解答の根拠となる部分は太字で示しています。**

⬇

❸ 英文全体の構文把握や意味を理解する

構文図解と全訳を参考にして、全文を理解します。**主語と動詞の把握、修飾語のカタマリと役割を把握**して、**全文の構文**を確認していきます。

⬇

❹ 知らない単語を必ず覚える

語彙リストを利用して、**英語・日本語セットで3回書いて、10回唱えてください。**単語学習のコツは、何度も繰り返すことです。

⬇

❺ 音声を聞きながら、後に続けて音読を10回する

音声を右ページを参考にダウンロードして、**音声に合わせて、テキストを見ながら10回音読**をします。**句や節といった意味の切れ目を意識して音読**してください。10回目に近付くにつれて、**英語を英語のまま理解できるいわゆる英語脳に近付く**ことができます。**③と④の工程をしっかりやること**が、**スムーズに音読できる最大のコツ**であることを覚えておいてください。

本シリーズのレベル設定

本シリーズは、現状の学力に見合った学習を促すために、下記の表のように、細かいレベル分けをしています。

レベル	対象
スタンダードレベル	**日本大、東洋大、駒沢大、専修大**や、**京都産業大、近畿大、甲南大、龍谷大などに代表される私立大学**を目指す人、**共通テストでの平均点以上**や**地方国公立大**を目指す人。
ハイレベル	**学習院大、明治大、青山学院大、立教大、中央大、法政大**や、**関西大、関西学院大、同志社大、立命館大などの難関私大**を目指す人。**共通テストでの高得点や上位国公立大**を目指す人。
トップレベル	**早稲田大、慶応大、上智大、東京理科大**などの**最難関私大**を目指す人。**共通テストで満点**や、**北大、東北大、東京大、名古屋大、京都大、大阪大、九州大などの難関国公立大**を目指す人。

難易度のレベルには変動があり、あくまでも目安です。

音声ダウンロードの方法

ヘッドフォンマークの中の番号は音声ファイル内のトラック番号です。

パソコンかスマートフォンで、
右のQRコードを読み取るか

https://kanki-pub.co.jp/pages/ghsaishinh/

にアクセスして、音声ファイルをダウンロードしてください。

※音声ダウンロードについてのお問合せ先：https://kanki-pub.co.jp/pages/infodl/

本編に入る前に

● 句と節について

句と節とは、両方とも**意味のカタマリ**と思っていただいて大丈夫です。例えば、When he woke up, the class was over.では、When he woke upまでが1つの意味のカタマリで、そこにhe woke upという**SVの文構造があると、節**といいます。かつWhen he woke upはwasを修飾する副詞の働きをしているので、**副詞節**といいます。

また、I like to read comics.という文では、to read comicsが「漫画を読むこと」という意味のカタマリを作っており、そこに**SVがないので、句**といいます。かつto read comicsは「漫画を読むこと」という名詞のカタマリなので、**名詞句**といいます。

節は、**名詞節・形容詞節・副詞節**、句は**名詞句・形容詞句・副詞句**と、意味のカタマリで分類すると、6種類があります。

● カッコについて

名詞のカタマリ（**名詞句・名詞節**）は〈　　〉で表します。**形容詞のカタマリ**（**形容詞句・形容詞節**）は（　　）で表し、前の名詞を修飾します。**副詞のカタマリ**（**副詞句・副詞節**）は［　　］で表し、動詞を修飾します。

● 文の要素について

英文の各パーツを理解するために、**S**（**主語**）、**V**（**動詞**）、**O**（**目的語**）、**C**（**補語**）、**M**（**修飾語**）という5つの要素に振り分けます。無理にこの5つに当てはめないほうがいい場合は、何も記号を振りません。

Sは、I go to school.のIのような**日本語の「～は・が」に当たる部分**です。**V**は、goのような**日本語の「～する」に当たる部分**です。**O**はI like soccer.のsoccerのような**動詞の目的語**です。**C**は、I am a teacher.のa teacherのように、**主語やときに目的語の補足説明**をする部分です。

● 品詞について

名詞・形容詞・副詞・前置詞が役割をおさえるべき主要な品詞です。**名詞**は、I like soccer.のように、Iという名詞が**文のS**になったり、soccerという名詞が**文のO**になったり、I am a teacher.のa teacherのように**C**になります。**名詞は文のS・O・C**のいずれかになります。

形容詞は、a cute girlのcuteのように**名詞を修飾**するか、He is old.のoldのように**補語**になります。**形容詞は、名詞を修飾するか文の補語になる**かのいずれかです。

副詞は、very goodのveryのように、うしろの**副詞や形容詞を修飾**します。You can see the world clearly.のclearlyのように「はっきりと見える」と**動詞を修飾**したり、Clearly, you need to exercise.のClearlyのように「明らかに、あなたは運動する必要がある」と、**文を修飾**したりします。**副詞は名詞以外の形容詞・副詞・動詞・文を修飾**します。

前置詞は、The train for Osaka will arrive at nine.のforのように、for Osaka「大阪行きの」という**形容詞のカタマリを作って前の名詞The trainを修飾**したり、atのようにat nine「9時に」という**副詞のカタマリを作って動詞arriveを修飾**したりします。**前置詞は形容詞のカタマリと副詞のカタマリ**を作ります。

● 具体と抽象について

抽象とは、簡単に言うと、**まとめ・まとまり**のことです。それを**具体例**を用いて、わかりやすく説明していくのが、英語に最もよく見られる論理展開です。例えば、
「彼は、**複数の言語**を話すことができる」
「例えば、**日本語・英語・中国語**など」
上の例では、「**(彼の話すことのできる)複数の言語**」が**抽象表現**に当たり、**「日本語・英語・中国語」**が**具体例**です。このつながりが見えてくると、英語長文の理解がグンと深まります。

● 因果関係について

因果関係とは、**原因と結果の関係**のことです。英語の世界では、**こういった原因から、この結果が生まれたという因果関係をとても重要視**します。例えば、「昨日とても夜遅くに寝た」という原因から、「今日はとても眠い」という結果が生まれます。

● パラフレーズについて

本書では、**パラフレーズ(言い換え)**という用語を多用しています。本来は、phrase「句」という一定の意味のカタマリの言い換えに使いますが、本書では**単語の言い換え、文の言い換えにまで幅広くパラフレーズという用語を使っている**ので、ご承知おきください。

● 関係詞について

関係代名詞(which, who, that, what)と**関係副詞**(when, where, why, how)があります。基本は、**形容詞のカタマリを作って前の名詞を説明する働き**です。例えば、
This is the book **which** I like the best.
「これは私がいちばん好きな本です」
のように、the bookにwhich以下が説明を加えます。

● 不定詞について

to ＋ 動詞の原形 を不定詞といいます。S・O・Cで使う**名詞的用法「～すること」**、名詞を修飾する**形容詞的用法「～する（ための）」**、動詞を修飾する**副詞的用法「～するために」**があります。例えば、

I want something hot **to drink**.

「温かい飲み物がほしい」

の**to drink**が**不定詞の形容詞的用法**で、something hot「温かいもの」を修飾しています。

● 分詞と分詞構文について

分詞には、**現在分詞**（doing）と**過去分詞**（done）があります。**形容詞として使用**すると、the window **broken** by the boy「その少年が割った窓」のように、**名詞の後ろにおいて説明を加えます**。

一方で、**分詞を副詞として使用**すると、**分詞構文**になります。全部で3パターンあり、① Doing（Done）～, SV.、② S, doing（done）～, V.、③ SV ～, doing（done）.... です。例えば、

Seeing his parents, he ran away.

「両親を見ると、彼は逃げ去った」

のSeeing ～が分詞構文で、「～すると」と接続詞の意味を補って訳します。

問題 1

健康

睡眠不足

別冊 p.2 ／制限時間 20 分／ 398 words

解答

A. ウ　B. イ

C. 全体として見ると、すべての先進国の成人の２人につき１人が、次の１週間に必要とする睡眠をとらないだろう。

D. 私たちは罰則なしでは負債をためることはできないし、後になってその睡眠負債を返済することもできない。

E. ① ウ　③ オ　⑤ ア

解説

A.

ア．アメリカの成人のほぼ30％が、ほとんどの人よりも睡眠時間が少ない

イ．アメリカの成人のほぼ30％が、一晩につき６時間以上睡眠をとる

ウ．アメリカの成人のほぼ30％が、一晩につき６時間かそれ以下しか睡眠をとっていない

エ．アメリカの成人のうち、100年前の人より多く眠っているのは30％しかいない

下線部(1)は、**代動詞の do** がポイント。**代動詞の do** は、**前出の動詞＋目的語などの代わり**ができる。ここでの do は、sleep six hours or less a night のことなので、**ウ. nearly 30 percent of American adults get six hours or less of sleep a night** が正解。**本文の almost が選択肢では nearly にパラフレーズされている**ことに注意する。

B.

ア．よい状況が現れる

イ．その状況は似たように見える

ウ．私たちは世界をもっとよく見ることができる

エ．私たちは物事をはっきりと見ることができる

下線部(2)は、**things**が「**状況**」を意味する名詞。**no better**は**no＋比較級**に注意する。

構文 POINT ❶ no＋比較級は2つの役割

no＋比較級の表現は、**比較級になっている形容詞や副詞の意味を反転**させて、**イコールの関係**を作ります。以下の例文をご覧ください。
（例文）
This camera is **no bigger than** my hand.
訳 このカメラは私の手ほどの大きさしかない。

後ろの意味を反転させるので、**bigger（原級はbig）をsmall**とします。イコールの関係はas ～ as... で表すので、**no bigger than ＝ as small as「～と同程度に小さい」**となります。

本問ではno betterなので、better（原級はgood）の意味を反転させてbadとして、イコールの関係をas ～ as...で表すと、**as bad as...**となる。2個目のas以下が省略されているが、すでに登場した**the U.S.が省略されている**と考えて、「**状況はアメリカと同様にひどい**」と解釈する。よって、**イ. the situations appear similarが正解**とわかる。

C.

構文図解

[Taken as a whole], one (out of every two adults) (across all developed countries) will not get the necessary sleep (they need this coming week).

Taken(分詞構文) as a whole: M / one: S / out of every two adults: M / across all developed countries: M（adultsを指す） / will not get: V / the necessary sleep: O / (関係詞の省略) they need this coming week: M

Taken as a wholeで**分詞構文**の意味のカタマリになる。takeは「とらえる」の意味で、**as a whole**が「**全体として**」なので、「全体としてとらえると」＝「全体として見ると」とする。続いて、**A out of B「Bの中のA」**なので、「**2人の成人につき1人**」と訳す。acrossから前置詞のカタマリが始まって、countriesまでの形容詞句を作り、every two adultsを修飾している。

続いて、will not getがV、the necessary sleepがOで、第3文型とわかる。sleep they needで 名詞 **SVの並び**から**関係詞の省略**とわかるので、they ~ weekの形容詞節がsleepを修飾する。まとめると、「**全体としてみると、すべての先進国の成人2人につき1人が、次の1週間に必要な睡眠をとらないだろう**」となる。

D.

構文図解

norの後ろの倒置

We(S) cannot accumulate(V) a debt(O) [without penalty](M), nor can we(S) repay(V) that sleep debt(O) [at a later time](M).

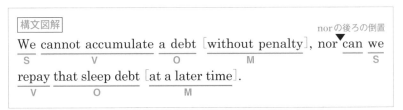

まずは、**cannot A without B「Bなしでは A できない」**の**二重否定**に注意する。続いて、norは**否定文**を受けて、**~, nor ... .「~ではない、また…ない」**と使う。…が**疑問文の語順**で、can we repayとなっていることに注意する。まとめると「**私たちは罰則なしでは負債をためることはできないし、後になってその睡眠負債を返済することもできない**」となる。

構文 POINT ❷ norやsoの後ろの倒置に注意する

norやsoの後ろでは倒置することがあるので、注意しましょう。
(例文)
I don't know the truth, **nor do I want** to.
訳 私は真実を知らないし、知りたいとも思わない。
I was happy and **so were the others**.
訳 私は幸せだったし、他の人もそうだった。

~, nor ... .「**~ではない、また…ない**」の…に**倒置が起きて疑問文の語順**になります。上の例文ではknow the truthがtoの後ろに省略されています。

soは肯定文を受けて、**~, so ... .**「**~だ、また…だ**」となります。下の例文では、soの後ろは、**were the others happyと疑問文の語順**になり、happyが省略されています。

E.

空所を含む文は、Would altering sleep attitudes and increasing sleep amounts (5) (①) any (②) (③) (④) (⑤) as a human race, to our professions and corporations, to commercial productivity, to salaries, the education of our children, or even our moral nature? である。**altering と increasing が動名詞**で、**altering sleep attitudes「睡眠に対する考えを改めること」**と**increasing sleep amounts「睡眠時間を増やすこと」**が文のSになる。すると、次に置くべきなのはVなので、ウのmakeとイのdifferenceを①、②に使って、**make any difference「違いを作り出す」**とする。

続いて、「何に」違いを作り出すのかを考えて、**to our collective lives「私たちの集団生活に」**として、③~⑤にオ・エ・アと順に並べる。まとめると、**make** any **difference to our collective lives**が完成された英文となる。よって、①、③、⑤に入る正解は、**ウ**、**オ**、**ア**となる。

構文図解

A hundred years ago, less than 2 percent (of the population in the United States) slept six hours or less a night. Now, almost 30 percent (of American adults) do. The lens (of a 2013 survey) (by the National Sleep Foundation) pulls this sleep deficiency [into sharp focus]. More than 65 percent (of the US adult population) fail to obtain the recommended seven to nine hours (of sleep) each night [during the week]. Circumnavigate the globe, and things look no better. [In the UK and Japan], [for example], 39 and 66 percent, respectively, (of all adults) report sleeping [fewer than seven hours]. Sleep neglect is common [throughout all developed nations], and it is for these reasons that the World Health Organization now labels the lack of societal sleep as a global health epidemic. [Taken as a whole], one (out of every two adults) (across all developed countries) will not get the necessary sleep (they need this coming week).

Importantly, many (of these individuals) do not report 〈wanting or needing less sleep〉. [If you look at sleep time in the developed nations for the weekends], the numbers are very different. [Rather than a mere 30 percent of adults getting eight hours of sleep or more on average], almost 60 percent (of these individuals) attempt to catch up on eight or more hours (of lost sleep).

sleep six hours or less a nightの代わり
6時間以下の睡眠時間の人が多いこと
命令文, and ... .「～しなさい、そうすれば…」
睡眠不足が世界中に蔓延していること
it is A that ～.「～なのはAだ」(強調構文)
label A as B「AをBとみなす」のas
分詞構文
adultsを指す
関係詞の省略
動名詞
睡眠不足の人たち
現在分詞の後置修飾

本文訳

100年前は、毎晩6時間かそれ以下しか眠らない人は、アメリカ人の2パーセントに満たない程度だった。今や、アメリカの成人のほぼ30%が、毎晩6時間以下しか眠らない。全米睡眠協会の2013年の調査は、この睡眠不足を詳しく解明している。アメリカの成人の65%以上が、1週間のうちのどの晩も推奨（すいしょう）されている7～9時間の睡眠をとれていない。世界的に見ても、状況は同様に全然よくないようだ。例えば、イギリスや日本では、全成人のそれぞれ39%、66%が、7時間未満の睡眠時間を報告している。睡眠を軽視することは、すべての先進国で共通のことであり、世界保健機関が、社会的な睡眠不足を健康面での世界的な流行とみなすのは、こうした理由からだ。全体として見ると、すべての先進国の成人の2人につき1人が、次の1週間に必要とする睡眠をとらないだろう。

重要なことは、こうした睡眠不足の人の多くが、少ない睡眠時間を望む、あるいは少ない睡眠時間で問題ないとは報告していないことだ。もしあなたが先進国の週末の睡眠時間を見るなら、その数字は全然違うものになる。平均8時間かそれ以上の睡眠をとる30%程度の成人よりもむしろ、睡眠不足の人のほぼ60%が、8時間かそれ以上の不足分の睡眠を取り戻そうとしている。

語彙リスト

population	名	人口
lens	名	レンズ
survey	名	調査
pull A into B	熟	AをBに動かす
deficiency	名	不足
sharp	形	はっきりした
focus	名	焦点
fail to do	熟	～しない
obtain	動	手に入れる
recommend	動	すすめる
sleep	名	睡眠
circumnavigate	動	一周する
no better	熟	少しもよくない
respectively	副	それぞれ
neglect	名	軽視
label A as B	熟	AをBとみなす
societal	形	社会の
epidemic	名	流行
as a whole	熟	全体として
A out of B	熟	Bの中のA
individual	名	個人
weekend	名	週末
rather than	熟	～よりむしろ
on average	熟	平均して
attempt to do	熟	～しようとする
catch up on	熟	～を取り返す

▶単語10回CHECK 1 2 3 4 5 6 7 8 9 10

構文図解

Each weekend, (vast numbers of) people are desperately trying to pay back a sleep debt (they've built up during the week). However, [as we have learned time and again], sleep is not [like a credit system or the bank]. The brain can never recover all the sleep (it has been deprived of). We cannot accumulate a debt [without penalty], nor can we repay that sleep debt [at a later time].

M M S V O 関係詞の省略 vast numbers of peopleを指す M M 様態のas「～ように」 M 「何度も」 S V 前置詞のlike M S V O The brainを指す norの後ろの倒置 M S V O M S V O M

[Beyond any single individual], why should society care? Would 〈altering sleep attitudes and increasing sleep amounts〉 make any difference [to our collective lives as a human race], [to our professions and corporations], [to commercial productivity], [to salaries, the education of our children, or even our moral nature]? [Whether you are a business leader or employee, the director of a hospital, a practicing doctor or nurse, a government official or military person, a public-policy maker or community health worker, anyone who expects to receive any form of medical care at any moment in their life, or a parent], the answer is very much "yes," [for more reasons] [than you may imagine].

M M S V 動名詞 S altering ～とincreasing ～の接続 V O M M M M salaries, the education of our children, our moral natureの接続 M whether A or B whether A or B whether A or B whether A or B whether A or B S V C M M

本文訳

毎週末、膨大な数の人が、週の間にため込んだ睡眠負債を必死になって返そうとしている。しかし、私たちが何度も学んだように、睡眠はクレジットカードや銀行のようなものとは違う。脳は、取り損ねた睡眠すべてを取り返すことは決してできない。私たちは罰則なしでは負債をためることはできないし、後になってその睡眠負債を返済することもできない。

一個人を越えて、なぜ社会が注意すべきなのか。睡眠に対する考えを改めて、睡眠時間を増やせば、人類としての私たちの集団生活、また、私たちの仕事や企業、商業上の生産性、給料、子供の教育、あるいは人の道徳心にまで違いをもたらすだろうか。あなたが経営者であろうと従業員であろうと、病院の院長、開業医、看護師、政府の役人や軍人、政策立案者や地域保健員などであろうと、人生のいかなる時に何らかの医療を受けようと思っているだれであろうと親であろうと、答えはあなたの想像以上に多くの理由で、絶対に「イエス」である。

語彙リスト

vast	形 膨大な
desperately	副 必死になって
pay back	熟 返す
debt	名 負債
build up	熟 増やす
time and again	熟 何度も
deprive A of B	熟 AからBを奪う
accumulate	動 ～を蓄積する
penalty	名 処罰
repay	動 返済する
alter	動 変える
attitude	名 考え
amount	名 量
make a difference	熟 違いを作る
collective	形 集団の
human race	名 人類
profession	名 職業
corporation	名 企業
commercial	形 商業上の
productivity	名 生産性
salary	名 給料
employee	名 従業員
director	名 局長
practice	動 開業する
government official	名 政府の役人
military	形 軍の
medical care	名 医療

▸単語10回CHECK 1 2 3 4 5 6 7 8 9 10

A hundred years ago, less than 2 percent of the population in the United States slept six hours or less a night. Now, almost 30 percent of American adults do. The lens of a 2013 survey by the National Sleep Foundation pulls this sleep deficiency into sharp focus. More than 65 percent of the US adult population fail to obtain the recommended seven to nine hours of sleep each night during the week. Circumnavigate the globe, and things look no better. In the UK and Japan, for example, 39 and 66 percent, respectively, of all adults report sleeping fewer than seven hours. Sleep neglect is common throughout all developed nations, and it is for these reasons that the World Health Organization now labels the lack of societal sleep as a global health epidemic. Taken as a whole, one out of every two adults across all developed countries will not get the necessary sleep they need this coming week.

Importantly, many of these individuals do not report wanting or needing less sleep. If you look at sleep time in the developed nations for the weekends, the numbers are very different. Rather than a mere 30 percent of adults getting eight hours of sleep or more on average, almost 60 percent of these individuals attempt to catch up on eight or more hours of lost sleep. Each weekend, vast numbers of people are desperately trying to pay back a sleep debt they've built up during the week. However, as we have learned time and again, sleep is not like a credit system or the bank. The brain can never recover all the sleep it has been deprived of. We cannot accumulate a debt without penalty, nor can we repay that sleep debt at a later time.

Beyond any single individual, why should society care? Would altering sleep attitudes and increasing sleep amounts make any difference to our collective lives as a human race, to our professions and corporations, to commercial productivity, to salaries, the education of our children, or even our moral nature? Whether you are a business leader or employee, the director of a hospital, a practicing doctor or nurse, a government official or military person, a public-policy maker or community health worker, anyone who expects to receive any form of medical care at any moment in their life, or a parent, the answer is very much "yes," for more reasons than you may imagine.

▶音読10回CHECK 1 2 3 4 5 6 7 8 9 10

背景知識が広がるコラム

BACKGROUND KNOWLEDGE

しっかりした睡眠をとる方法

現代社会は**ストレス社会**とも言うべき時代で、**心の問題**がいろいろなところで問題視されています。そして、その**心の問題と睡眠は密接な関係**にあります。いわゆる**うつ症状には、不眠症が関係**していることがあり、**しっかりした睡眠をとることは、心の健康を保つのにも重要**になります。では、しっかりした睡眠をとるために、何をすればよいのでしょうか。

まずは、**午前中に太陽の光を浴びて、リズム運動をすること**が重要です。リズム運動とは、歩くこと、ジョギングなどの有酸素運動を指します。これにより、幸せホルモンと言われる**セロトニンが活性化**します。このセロトニンがもとで、**睡眠ホルモンと言われるメラトニンが生成されて、夜の睡眠を促します。**

続いて、**晩御飯を就寝の3時間前に終わらせて、一定量の炭水化物を摂取すること**で、夜ぐっすり眠れるようになります。糖質制限が流行している昨今ですが、**夜に炭水化物を抜くと、しばらくするといわゆる不眠症に陥ってしまいます。晩御飯に一定量の炭水化物をとることが、安眠へと導いてくれます。**

そして、夕方からの**入浴習慣はよい睡眠を導いてくれること**があります。入浴により体温を上昇させて、緩やかに体温を下降させていくことで入眠へと導いてくれます。ただし、**就寝直前の熱いお風呂は、覚醒して体温が不安定になるので逆効果**になります。

最後に、**夜間に携帯やパソコンの強い光を避けること**も重要です。携帯電話やパソコンから発せられる**ブルーライト**が**長時間目に当たると、目の疲れに加え、体内リズムを崩し睡眠障害を引き起こす**ことが報告されています。太陽光にも非常に強いブルーライトが含まれており、午前中に浴びるブルーライトは問題ないのですが、夜間に浴びると不眠症の原因となってしまいます。対策としては、**携帯やパソコンの液晶の光を抑えて**、日常的にブルーライトを抑えます。続いて、**就寝の最低2時間前にはパソコンの使用を控える**、そして**30分前には携帯電話の使用も控える**とよいでしょう。**しっかりした睡眠が、心身の安定、集中力の向上、ストレスの軽減や円滑な人間関係など、すべてにプラスの影響**をもたらします。

問題 2

心理

心の知能指数

別冊p.6／制限時間25分／491 words

解答

Question1	a T	b T	c F	d F	e F	
Question2	1 a	2 f	3 e	4 h	5 g	6 b
Question3	Ⅰ e	Ⅱ d	Ⅲ a			

解説

Question1

以下の表現が正しいか間違っているかを特定しなさい。解答欄にTかFと書きなさい。

a　EQは時間を経て変化する可能性がある。

第2段落第3文 ~, you can increase your emotional intelligence from whatever level it is today.「~、**現在の感情知能がどんな段階であっても、それを高めることはできる**」と合致するので、**T**。

b　経営者はたいてい高い感情知能を備えている。

第4段落第2文 ~, 75 percent of top managers in Germany, Latin America and Japan possess high EQ.「~、**ドイツ、ラテンアメリカ、日本のトップ経営者の75%が高いEQを保有している**」と合致するので、**T**。

語彙 POINT ❶　「所有する(保有する)」のパラフレーズ

「**所有する**」のパラフレーズは頻出なので、確実におさえておきましょう。いちばん簡単な「**所有する**」が**have**で、**own, possess**と続きます。

本問のように、本文ではpossessが使われていたのが、選択肢ではhaveにパラフレーズされているのに気づけば、容易に正解に至る。

c 女性は全般的に男性より高いEQを備えている。

第5段落第1文～, each gender tends to demonstrate higher EQ in specific areas「～、どちらの性別も、特定の分野でより高いEQを示す傾向にある」とあるだけで、**女性が全般的に男性より高いという記述はないので、F。**

d 人々は長い間EQを研究し続けている。

第6段落第1文 The field is relatively young, scientifically speaking, and more research is being done that has fueled some controversy.「この分野は、科学的には、比較的歴史が浅く、さらなる研究が行われている最中であり、これまで何らかの議論も生まれてきた」と反するので、F。and以下に**分離**が起きているので注意する。

構文 POINT ❸ 分離

(例文)

The time will come **when we can travel to the moon.**

訳 月に旅行できる時代がやってくるだろう。

名詞と修飾する不定詞句や関係詞節が離れる現象を**分離**といいます。例文では、元々The timeを修飾していたwhen ～ moonが、主語が長くなるので、分離してcomeの後ろに回りました。

and以下の文は、元々more research **that has fueled some controversy** is being doneの**that ～ controversy**が**分離**して後ろに回り、more research is being done **that has fueled some controversy**となっている。

e EQを計測するのは簡単だ。

第6段落第2文～, measuring "human effectiveness at managing relationships" is bound to cause difficulties.「『対人関係を管理する人間の有効性』を計測することは、必ず困難をもたらすものだ」に反するので、**F**。第2段落第1文から、human effectiveness at managing relationshipsがEQと同義であることに注意する。

1 健康 2 心理 3 IT・テクノロジー 4 健康 5 IT・テクノロジー 6 IT・テクノロジー 7 環境 8 文化 9 環境 10 社会

Question2

下線部の単語(1)～(6)と似ている意味の言葉を選びなさい。解答欄の空白に(a)～(i)を記入しなさい。それぞれ一度しか使用できない。

(a) 順応する　(b) 難しい　(c) 寛大な
(d) 修正する　(e) 肯定的な　(f) およそ
(g) まき散らす　(h) 刺激する　(i) 強い

1

adaptは「**適応する**」の意味で、**(a) adjust**「**順応する**」が似ているので、正解となる。

語彙 POINT ❷ **adaptとadjustの覚え方**

adaptとadjustはスペリングが似ているので語源を利用して覚えましょう。adaptは、**apt**「**適した**」に着目します。動詞になると「**適した状態になる**」＝「**適応する**」になります。adjustは**just**「**ちょうど**」に着目します。動詞になると「**ちょうどよい状態になる**」＝「**順応する**」になります。

2

approximatelyは、簡単な単語に直すと**about**「**およそ**」**と一緒**で、本問では **(f) roughly**「**およそ**」が正解になる。

語彙 POINT ❸ **難しい副詞のパラフレーズ**

難しい副詞	意味	簡単な単語
approximately	およそ	about
frequently	頻繁に	often
currently	現在	now

難しい副詞を、簡単な単語に置き換えて覚えると、パラフレーズの問題に強くなります。本問の**approximately**は**about**、**frequently**「**頻繁に**」は**often**、**currently**「**現在**」は**now**と同じと覚えましょう。

3

optimistic「**楽観的な**」の意味から、(e) **positive**「**肯定的な**」が正解。**opt**「**選ぶ**」と語源が同じなので、**"自ら選んだ"というプラスイメージ**から、「**楽観的な**」を連想する。

4

fuelは通常、名詞では「**燃料**」の意味だが、動詞で使われると「**燃料を補給する**」=「**あおる**」の意味から、(h) **stimulate**「**刺激する**」が正解。

5

pepperは通常、名詞では「**コショウ**」の意味。動詞で使われると、「**コショウを振りかける**」=「**散りばめる**」になるので、(g) **sprinkle**「**まき散らす**」が正解。

6

tough「**困難な**」という意味から、(b) **difficult**が正解。

Question3

空欄Ⅰ～Ⅲに最も適切な見出しを選びなさい。

(a) 他人の感情や業績に理解ある反応を示す
(b) あなたの同僚との対人関係を改善する
(c) 具体的な事実の情報に集中する
(d) ボディランゲージから感情のヒントを探す
(e) 聞くことの潜在的な障壁となるものを意識する
(f) 常に真実を言う

Ⅰ

1.の下の表現は、**Effective listening improves every relationship, and you'd be surprised how much better others listen after they've truly been heard.**「**しっかりと聞くことはすべての関係性をよくするし、他人の話をしっかり聞いた後では、その人たちがどれほどしっかりと聞いてくれるかに驚くだろう**」から、**しっかりと人の話を聞くことの重要性に関するテーマ**とわかる。よって、(e) **Be aware of potential listening blocks**が正解。

1 健康 2 心理 3 IT・テクノロジー 4 健康 5 IT・テクノロジー 6 IT・テクノロジー 7 環境 8 文化 9 環境 10 社会

Ⅱ

2.の下の表現は、**Beyond the obvious — tears of sadness or joy, for example — see if you can tell what someone is feeling simply by the way they are carrying themselves.**「**例えば悲しみの涙や喜びの涙のような明白なもの以外に、ある人がふるまうそのふるまい方だけで、その人が何を感じているのかがわかるか確かめよう**」から、**人のふるまいからその人の感情を読み取ることに関するテーマ**とわかる。よって、**(d) Look for emotional clues in body language**が正解。ちなみに、本文の**carry oneself**は「**ふるまう**」の意味の表現。

Ⅲ

3.の下の表現は、**Pepper your conversations with sincere, empathetic lines such as, "That must have been tough," or, "You sound like you really enjoyed that."**「**あなたの会話に『それは大変だったね』とか『本当に楽しかったようだね』などの誠実で、共感的なセリフを散りばめなさい**」から、**(a) Reflect others' feelings and achievements with supportive feedback**が正解。

1 健康
2 心理
3 IT・テクノロジー
4 健康
5 IT・テクノロジー
6 IT・テクノロジー
7 環境
8 文化
9 環境
10 社会

構文図解

Are you familiar with EQ, or "Emotional Intelligence"? [Even as of 2004], less than 25 percent (of our seminar participants) said, yes. This surprised me, [since Emotional Intelligence, first popularized by Daniel Goleman in 1995, is a fire that spread well beyond its initial spark among the personal and professional development industries]. Let's fan the flames.

V S V O 同格のor「すなわち」 M
EQを知っている人が25%以下だったこと S M V O
S V O 理由のsince M 分詞構文
関係代名詞のthat
V O

What is EQ?

Daniel Goleman defines EQ as "The ability to manage ourselves and our relationships effectively." I think of EQ as "IQ of the heart." But [whereas your IQ (intelligence quotient) rarely, if ever, improves with age], you can increase your emotional intelligence [from whatever level it is today]. And you can increase your staff's emotional intelligence, too.

S V A as B 不定詞 形容詞的用法
S V A as B
M 「するとしてもめったに～しない」
S V O M
your emotional intelligenceを指す S V O
M

Why Focus on EQ?

Would you like your staff to adapt more quickly to change and respond better to setbacks and obstacles? Four leading international companies reported 〈that EQ competencies account for approximately 80 percent of job performance〉. [If any one factor figures as much as this], it must at least be [worth a look].

S V O to do adaptとrespondの接続
S
V 名詞節のthat O
EQと同じくらい重要な要因 M
EQを指す S V M

本文訳

あなたは、EQ、すなわち「感情知能」のことをよく知っているだろうか？　2004年時点でさえ、私たちのセミナー参加者の25%以下しか「知っている」とは言わなかった。このことは私を驚かせた。それは、感情知能は1995年にダニエル・ゴールマンが最初に広めたもので、*自己啓発、そして職業訓練の分野で生じた初めの火花をはるかに超えて燃え広まった炎だからだ。その炎をもっとあおってみよう。

EQとは何か？

ダニエル・ゴールマンはEQを「自分自身や自分の対人関係を効果的に管理する能力」と定義する。私はEQを「心のIQ」とみなす。しかし、あなたのIQ（知能指数）は加齢とともによくなることはめったにないが、現在の感情知能がどんな段階であっても、それを高めることができる。そして、あなたのスタッフの感情知能を高めることもできる。

なぜEQに焦点を当てるか？

あなたは自分のスタッフに、もっと素早く変化に適応して、つまずきや障害にもっと上手に対応してもらいたいだろうか？　4つの国際的なトップの企業が、EQの能力によって、仕事の成果のおよそ80%の説明がつくと報告した。もしいかなる要因でも、EQと同じくらい重要なものが現れるなら、それは少なくとも一見の価値があるに違いない。

*「自己啓発」は、自分自身の能力向上や精神的な成長を目指すことを意味する。

語彙リスト

be familiar with	熟	～に精通している
as of	熟	～時点で
participant	名	参加者
popularize	動	～を普及させる
fire	名	火、炎
spread	動	広がる
initial	形	最初の
spark	名	火花
personal	形	個人的な
professional	形	職業の
fan the flame	熟	感情などをあおる
manage	動	管理する
relationship	名	関係
effectively	副	効果的に
think of A as B	熟	AをBとみなす
whereas	接	～だけれども
rarely, if ever, ～	熟	するとしてもめったに～しない
whatever 名詞	熟	～するどんな名詞でも
adapt to	熟	～に適応する
respond to	熟	～に対応する
setback	名	つまずき
obstacle	名	障害
leading	形	一流の
competency	名	能力
account for	熟	～を説明する
approximately	副	およそ
performance	名	成績
factor	名	要因
figure	動	(重要なものとして)現れる

▸単語10回CHECK 1 2 3 4 5 6 7 8 9 10

構文図解

EQ, Gender and Culture

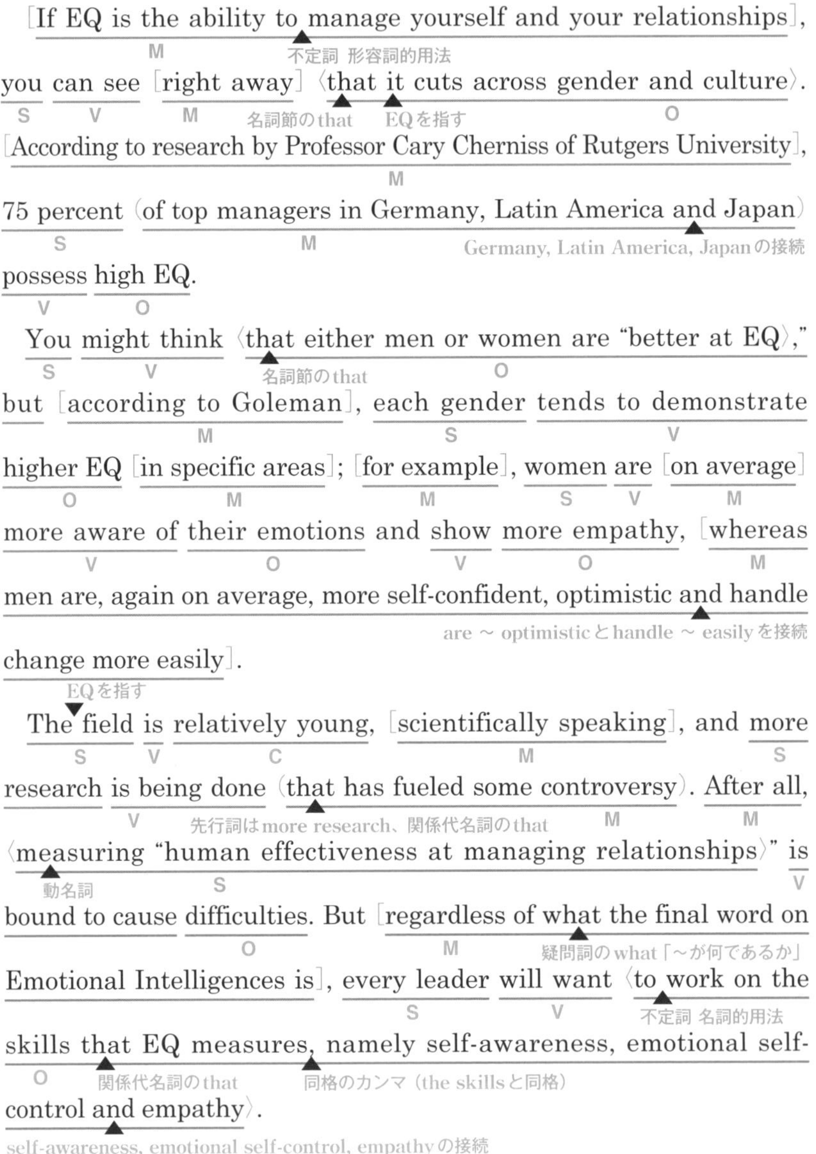

[If EQ is the ability to manage yourself and your relationships], you can see [right away] 〈that it cuts across gender and culture〉. [According to research by Professor Cary Cherniss of Rutgers University], 75 percent (of top managers in Germany, Latin America and Japan) possess high EQ.

You might think 〈that either men or women are "better at EQ〉," but [according to Goleman], each gender tends to demonstrate higher EQ [in specific areas]; [for example], women are [on average] more aware of their emotions and show more empathy, [whereas men are, again on average, more self-confident, optimistic and handle change more easily].

The field is relatively young, [scientifically speaking], and more research is being done (that has fueled some controversy). After all, 〈measuring "human effectiveness at managing relationships〉" is bound to cause difficulties. But [regardless of what the final word on Emotional Intelligences is], every leader will want 〈to work on the skills that EQ measures, namely self-awareness, emotional self-control and empathy〉.

本文訳

EQ、性別と文化

もしEQが自分とその対人関係を管理する能力なら、すぐにそれは性別や文化を超越(ちょうえつ)することがわかる。ラトガース大学のケリー・カーニス教授の研究によると、ドイツ、ラテンアメリカ、日本のトップ経営者の75%が高いEQを保有している。

男性か女性のどちらかがより「優れたEQ」を保有していると思うかもしれないが、ゴールマンによると、どちらの性別も、特定の分野でより高いEQを示す傾向にある。例えば、女性は平均して自分の感情をより理解していて、共感を示しやすいが、一方で男性は平均して、自信に満ちて、楽観的で、変化に対応するのがより簡単だ。

この分野は、科学的には、比較的歴史が浅く、さらなる研究が行われている最中で、これまで何らかの議論も生まれてきた。結局、「対人関係を管理する人間の有効性」を計測することは、必ず困難をもたらすものだ。しかし、感情知能の結論が何であるかに関係なく、すべてのリーダーは、EQで計測できるスキル、すなわち自己認識、自制心、そして共感能力に取り組みたいだろう。

語彙リスト

gender	名 性別
right away	熟 すぐに
cut across	熟 ～の領域を超える
possess	動 保有する
demonstrate	動 示す
specific	形 特定の
empathy	名 共感
self-confident	形 自信のある
optimistic	形 楽観的な
handle	動 扱う
relatively	副 比較的
scientifically	副 科学的に
fuel	動 あおる
controversy	名 議論
be bound to do	熟 必ず～する
regardless of	熟 ～に関係なく
work on	熟 ～に取り組む
measure	動 計測する
namely	副 すなわち
self-awareness	名 自己認識
self-control	名 自制心

▶単語10回CHECK 1 2 3 4 5 6 7 8 9 10

構文図解

Three Ways to Increase Your EQ Today

不定詞 形容詞的用法

[If you're interested in increasing your EQ], here are three tips:

M 動名詞 M V S

1. Be aware of potential listening blocks

V O

Effective listening improves every relationship, and you'd be surprised 〈how much better others listen after they've truly been heard〉.

S V O S V（you wouldの短縮形）

「どれほどよく～か」 比較級の強調 O othersを指す

2. Look for emotional clues 〈in body language〉

V O M

[Beyond the obvious] — tears of sadness or joy, for example — see 〈if you can tell what someone is feeling simply by the way they are carrying themselves〉. Are they bored? Worried? Watch a movie [with the sound off] [for a few minutes] and play a game [with others] [called "Spot the Emotion]." Professional actors have honed their skills [such that you should be able to tell what feelings they're expressing even without hearing their words].

M M V

名詞節のif「～かどうか」 疑問詞のwhat「何を～か」 O the way SV someoneを指す

V S C C V O

付帯状況のwith「OをCして」 M V O M

過去分詞の後置修飾（a gameを修飾） M S V

O 「とても（程度が）高いので…」 M 疑問形容詞「どんな名詞を～か」 professional actorsを指す

3. Reflect others' feelings and achievements [with supportive feedback]

V O M

Pepper your conversations [with sincere, empathetic lines] 〈such as, "That must have been tough," or, "You sound like you really enjoyed that〉." 〈Doing so〉 shows your counterpart 〈that you're interested in both the factual and emotional content of their stories〉.

V O M M

相手の言ったこと 会話に共感を織り交ぜること

相手の言ったこと S V O_1 名詞節のthat O_2

本文訳

今日からEQを高める3つの方法

もしあなたがEQを高めることに興味があるなら、3つのヒントがある。

1. 聞くことを妨げる可能性のあるものを意識する
しっかりと聞くことはすべての関係性をよくするし、相手の話をしっかり聞いた後に、その人がどれほどしっかりとこちらの話を聞いてくれるかに驚くだろう。

2. ボディランゲージから感情のヒントを探す
例えば、悲しみの涙やうれし泣きのような明白なもの以外に、ある人のふるまいだけで、その人が何を感じているのかがわかるか確かめよう。彼らは退屈しているのか？　心配しているのか？　数分音を消して映画を見て、「感情あて」と呼ばれるゲームを他の人とやるとよい。プロの俳優たちは、演技力を高度に磨いているので、彼らの言葉を聞かなくても、どんな感情を表現しているのかを伝えられる。

3. 他人の感情や成果に理解ある反応を示す
あなたの会話に「それは大変だったね」とか「本当に楽しかったようだね」などの誠実で、共感的なセリフを散りばめなさい。そうすることで、話し相手に、彼らの話の事実関係と感情面の両方に興味があると示すことができる。

語彙リスト

tip	名	ヒント
potential	形	潜在的な
block	名	障害
clue	名	ヒント
beyond the obvious	熟	明白なもの以外に
tear	名	涙
sadness	名	悲しみ
carry oneself	熟	ふるまう
spot	動	言いあてる
hone	動	磨きをかける
such that	熟	とても(程度が)高いので~
reflect	動	示す
supportive	形	理解のある
feedback	名	反応
pepper	動	散りばめる
conversation	名	会話
sincere	形	誠実な
empathetic	形	共感する
line	名	セリフ
tough	形	困難な
sound like	熟	～のように思える
counterpart	名	相対(あいたい)する人
factual	形	事実の
content	名	内容

▸単語10回CHECK　1　2　3　4　5　6　7　8　9　10

Are you familiar with EQ, or "Emotional Intelligence"? Even as of 2004, less than 25 percent of our seminar participants said, yes. This surprised me, since Emotional Intelligence, first popularized by Daniel Goleman in 1995, is a fire that spread well beyond its initial spark among the personal and professional development industries. Let's fan the flames.

What is EQ?

Daniel Goleman defines EQ as "The ability to manage ourselves and our relationships effectively." I think of EQ as "IQ of the heart." But whereas your IQ (intelligence quotient) rarely, if ever, improves with age, you can increase your emotional intelligence from whatever level it is today. And you can increase your staff's emotional intelligence, too.

Why Focus on EQ?

Would you like your staff to adapt more quickly to change and respond better to setbacks and obstacles? Four leading international companies reported that EQ competencies account for approximately 80 percent of job performance. If any one factor figures as much as this, it must at least be worth a look.

EQ, Gender and Culture

If EQ is the ability to manage yourself and your relationships, you can see right away that it cuts across gender and culture. According to research by Professor Cary Cherniss of Rutgers University, 75 percent of top managers in Germany, Latin America and Japan possess high EQ.

You might think that either men or women are "better at EQ," but according to Goleman, each gender tends to demonstrate higher EQ in specific areas; for example, women are on average more aware of their emotions and show more empathy, whereas men are, again on average, more self-confident, optimistic and handle change more easily.

The field is relatively young, scientifically speaking, and more research is being done that has fueled some controversy. After all, measuring "human effectiveness at managing relationships" is bound to cause difficulties. But regardless of what the final word on Emotional Intelligences is, every leader will want to work on the skills that EQ measures, namely self-awareness, emotional self-control and empathy.

Three Ways to Increase Your EQ Today

If you're interested in increasing your EQ, here are three tips:

1. Be aware of potential listening blocks

Effective listening improves every relationship, and you'd be surprised how much better others listen after they've truly been heard.

2. Look for emotional clues in body language

Beyond the obvious — tears of sadness or joy, for example — see if you can tell what someone is feeling simply by the way they are carrying themselves. Are they bored? Worried? Watch a movie with the sound off for a few minutes and play a game with others called "Spot the Emotion." Professional actors have honed their skills such that you should be able to tell what feelings they're expressing even without hearing their words.

3. Reflect others' feelings and achievements with supportive feedback

Pepper your conversations with sincere, empathetic lines such as, "That must have been tough," or, "You sound like you really enjoyed that." Doing so shows your counterpart that you're interested in both the factual and emotional content of their stories.

▸音読10回CHECK 1 2 3 4 5 6 7 8 9 10

BACKGROUND KNOWLEDGE

Emotional Intelligence

本問で登場したように、Emotional Intelligence Quotient「**感情的知能指数**」を略した"EQ"や"EI"という概念に注目が集まっています。IQ（Intelligence Quotient「**知能指数**」）が主に、**記憶力や集中力に基づいた学習能力の高さ**を示すのに対して、**EQ**は「**心の知能指数**」とも呼ばれるように、**感情面での知性の高低を数値化したもの**です。

EQとは、具体的には、**感情の動きを正確に認識する力、思考を促進するために感情の動きを利用する力、感情の動きの意味を理解する力、自分の感情を管理する、そして他者の感情に対応する能力**に分類できるとされます。

また、感情知能を広めた心理学者のダニエル・ゴールマン氏は、この概念を「**自己認識**」・「**自己管理**」・「**社会的認識**」・「**人間関係管理**」という、4つの"感情的能力"に分類しています。要するに、**"感情知能"**とは**自分と相手の感情を認識してその意味を理解すること**、そして**それぞれの感情の動きを利用して物事を進めること**、**自分の感情の動きを管理**して、**相手の感情の動きに対応する力**、とまとめることができるでしょう。

EQとは、いわゆる日本語で言う「**空気を読む力**」に近いものかもしれません。私も決して得意なほうではありませんが、それでも独りよがりにはなりたくないものです。

問題 3

IT・テクノロジー

顔認証システム

別冊p.10／制限時間20分／455 words

解答

問1 顔認証技術は、デジタルカメラで撮った画像に含まれている「生体データ」を人々の顔のデータと照合することで、個人の身元を特定する。

問2 大学はまた、長期間の欠席者を初期の段階で特定し、彼らに適切なカウンセリングが行われるように、この新しいシステムを利用することを望んでいる。

問3
1 It uses four tablets.
2 They should enter their identification numbers on the tablets for attendance registration.

問4 prevent nuisance related to checking attendance

問5 出席情報を教務システムに入力することだけでなく、生徒に出席カードを配布して回収する雑用から、教師が解放されるというメリットがある。

問1

構文図解

It (S) does (V) this (O) [by checking the “biometric data” contained in those camera images against people’s facial data] (M)

過去分詞の名詞修飾（contained ～ imagesまでの形容詞句）

check A against B「AをBと照合する」

ItがS、doesがV、thisがOの第3文型の文。**Itは前文の主語であるFacial recognition technology**を指す。

解法 POINT ❶ 指示語の特定

itやthisなどの指示語の特定は、基本は直前の文の同じ品詞を指します。あくまで原則ですが、指示語のitが主語で使われていたら、前の文の主語を指すのでは？　と考えます。

実際にこの文のItは**前文の主語のFacial recognition technology**を指している。**does this**は**前文のidentify or confirm an individual's personal identity**を指すので、「**個人の身元を特定する**」を意味する。続いて、**containedは過去分詞**で**imagesまでの形容詞句**を作り、**biometric dataを修飾**している。**check A against B**「**AをBと照合する**」が使われており、Aがthe "biometric data"で、Bがpeople's facial dataとなる。以上をまとめると、「**顔認証技術は、デジタルカメラで撮った画像に含まれている『生体データ』を人々の顔のデータと照合することで、個人の身元を特定する**」が正解。

問2

構文図解

The college also hopes 〈to utilize the new system to identify long-term absentees at an early stage so that appropriate counseling will be provided to them〉.

The college: S / also: M / hopes: V / 〈to utilize ... to them〉: O
to utilize: 不定詞 名詞的用法
to identify: 不定詞 副詞的用法
so that: so that S 助動詞
them: long-term absenteesを指す

The collegeがS、hopesがV、to utilize ～がOの第3文型の文。**to utilize ～は不定詞の名詞的用法**。to identifyは**不定詞の副詞的用法**で「～を特定するために」と訳す。

so that S 助動詞で「**Sが～するように**」という意味の副詞節を作り、utilizeを修飾している。最後のthemはlong-term absenteesを指す。以上をまとめると、「**大学はまた、長期間の欠席者を初期段階で特定し、彼らに適切なカウンセリングが行われるように、この新しいシステムを利用することを望んでいる**」となる。

問3

1 各教室で新しい出席システムに使用するタブレットは何台あるか？

解法 POINT ❷ **英問英答問題**

英問英答問題は、解答の該当箇所を探して微調整します。英問英答を見るだけで、最初は面食らってしまうかもしれませんが、実は非常に簡単な問題が多いものです。日本語の内容説明問題と同様に、解答する根拠に当たる該当箇所を探して、問題に合うように表現を調整すればよいだけなのです。

第3段落第1文**Sixteen** tablet devices ～ were introduced... , with four units ― ～ ― spread across **four lecture rooms.**から、**16台のタブレットが4つの講義室に分配**されたとあるので、**1つの教室に4台が割り当てられている**とわかる。よって、正解は**It（each classroom を指す）uses four tablets.**となる。

2 もしそのシステムが学生たちの顔を認識しないなら、彼らは何をすべきか？

第4段落第1文If the facial recognition functions do not work, students enter their identification numbers on the tablets for attendance registration.が解答の該当箇所とわかるので、**解答用に調整して、They（students を指す）should enter their identification numbers on the tablets for attendance registration.**が正解となる。

問4

(3)を含む文は、The system will help increase trust from students and parents in the college and (3) [attendance, nuisance, related, checking, prevent, to] in case classes are formed according to the levels of students' proficiency. となる。andが接続するものは、動詞のhelpかincreaseと推測できるので、(3)はpreventから始める。「**何を防ぐのか**」と考えて、**nuisance**「**面倒なこと**」をいったん目的語に置く。続いて、「**どんな面倒なことか**」を考えると、**relatedを過去分詞の後置修飾の働き**ととらえて、**related to checking attendance**「**出席を確認することにかかわる**」と並べると文意が通る。

以上をまとめると、**prevent nuisance related to checking attendance「出席を確認することにかかわる面倒なことを防ぐ」**が正解となる。欄外のandはincreaseとpreventを接続している。

問5

最終段落第1文が解答の該当箇所に適切なので、この文をまとめる。同段落第2文は、第1文の具体例なので、第1文のほうが解答にふさわしい。

構文図解

The facial recognition system (S) frees (V) teachers (O) [from the chore of handing out attendance cards to students and collecting them, as well as entering attendance information into the college's educational affairs system] (M).

and: handing ~ studentsとcollecting themの接続
them: attendance cardsを指す
as well as: B as well as A

The facial recognition systemがS、freesがV、teachersがOの第3文型の文。**free A from B「AをBから解放する」**の構文に注意する。andはhanding ~ studentsとcollecting themの接続。**B as well as A「AだけでなくBも」**に注意する。以上をまとめると、「**出席情報を大学の教務システムに入力することだけでなく、生徒に出席カードを配布して回収する雑用から、教師が解放されるというメリットがある**」が正解となる。

構文図解

過去分詞の名詞修飾

Facial recognition technology uses images (captured by digital

S　V　O　Facial recognition technology を指す

cameras) [to identify or confirm an individual's personal identity]. It

M　不定詞 副詞的用法　M　S

does this [by checking the "biometric data" contained in those camera

V　O　identify ～ identity を指す　M　過去分詞の名詞修飾 (contained ～ images までの形容詞句)

images against people's facial data (for example, size and shape of

check A against B　過去分詞の名詞修飾

face, eye color, etc.) contained in government or commercial

Facial recognition technology を指す

databases]. Today, it is most commonly used [in security systems]

不定詞 副詞的用法　M　S　V　M

[to check people for access to secure places, computers, or computer

M　Facial recognition technology を指す　places, computers, computer networks の接続

networks]. [In many countries], it is also increasingly used [by

M　S　V

government agencies — especially by police and other law

M　M

enforcement or public security agencies] — [for surveillance of

M

people's movements and activities in public areas].

Hyogo College (of Medicine) has introduced a facial recognition

S　M　V　Hyogo College of Medicine を指す

technology-based system [to check student attendance]. It is the first

O　不定詞 副詞的用法　M　S　V　C

university (in Japan) (to use such a system), [according to the

M　不定詞 形容詞的用法　M　M

institution in the city of Nishinomiya, Hyogo Prefecture]. The

S

university expects the system to allow teachers to check students'

V　O　to do　allow O to do の to do

attendance swiftly and accurately and improve the work efficiency of

allow ～と improve ～の接続

its staff who, until recently, had been using standard attendance

sheets.

本文訳

顔認証技術は、一人一人の身元を確認するのにデジタルカメルを使って撮った画像を利用する。政府や商業データベースに含まれる（例えば、顔の大きさや形、目の色などの）顔のデータと、デジタルカメラの画像に含まれている「生体データ」を照合することで、一人一人の身元を確認する。今日では、その技術は、安全な場所、コンピューター、あるいはコンピューターネットワークへアクセスする人を確認するために、セキュリティシステムにて、最もよく使われている。多くの国で、公共の場所での人の動きや活動を監視するのに、特に警察やその他の法執行機関や治安当局などの政府機関でますます使用されてもいる。

兵庫医科大学は、学生の出席を確認するために、顔認証技術に基づいたシステムを導入した。兵庫県の西宮市の担当課によると、兵庫医科大学はそのようなシステムを日本で最初に使用した大学だ。大学は、そのシステムによって、教師が学生の出席を迅速かつ正確に確認し、最近まで通常の出席シートを利用していた職員の業務効率を改善することができることを期待している。

語彙リスト

recognition	名 認識
image	名 画像
capture	動 読み取る
identify	動 特定する
confirm	動 確証する
identity	名 身元
check A against B	熟 AをBと照合する
biometric	形 生体識別の
contain	動 含んでいる
commercial	形 商業上の
secure	形 安全な
government agency	名 政府機関
especially	副 特に
law enforcement agency	名 法執行機関
introduce	動 導入する
attendance	名 出席
institution	名 組織
expect O to do	動 Oが~するのを期待する
swiftly	副 迅速に
accurately	副 正確に
efficiency	名 効率

▶単語10回CHECK 1 2 3 4 5 6 7 8 9 10

構文図解

Sixteen tablet devices (with facial recognition functions) were introduced [on Friday] last week, [with four units — one for teachers and three for students — spread across four lecture rooms]. The faces (of a total of some 470 students) had been registered [on the devices] beforehand. [At the start of classes], students register their attendance [using the tablets in turn]. The devices are held up [to their faces], and the images (shown on the displays) are checked [against the preregistered images].

付帯状況のwith　unitを指す　with O CのC　分詞構文　過去分詞の後置修飾

[If the facial recognition functions do not work], students enter their identification numbers [on the tablets] [for attendance registration]. Teachers can check the attendance [on their tablets], which show images (of students) [conducting the facial recognition process in real time]. The college also hopes ⟨to utilize the new system to identify long-term absentees at an early stage so that appropriate counseling will be provided to them⟩.

「(そして) それは」　分詞構文「そして～」　不定詞 名詞的用法　不定詞 副詞的用法　so that S 助動詞　long-term absenteesを指す

The facial recognition system frees teachers [from the chore of handing out attendance cards to students and collecting them, as well as entering attendance information into the college's educational affairs system].

同格のof「～という」　handing ～ studentsとcollecting themの接続　attendance cardsを指す　B as well as A

本文訳

顔認証機能を搭載した16のタブレット機器が先週金曜日に導入され、１つは教師用、３つは学生用として、４台ずつ４つの講義室に配置された。合計およそ470人の学生の顔が、前もってその機器に登録されていた。授業の始めに、学生は順番にタブレットを利用して、その出席を登録する。その機器は、顔の位置に掲げられ、ディスプレイに映された画像が、事前登録された画像と照合される。

もし顔認証機能が作動しないなら、学生は出席登録のためにタブレット上にID番号を入力する。教師は自分のタブレット上で出席を確認することができて、リアルタイムで顔認識をしながら、学生の画像を映し出す。大学はまた、長期間の欠席者を初期段階で特定し、彼らに適切なカウンセリングが行われるように、この新しいシステムを利用することを望んでいる。

顔認証システムによって、出席情報を教務システムに入力することだけでなく、生徒に出席カードを配布して回収する雑用から、教師は解放されている。

語彙リスト

device	名 機器
function	名 機能
unit	名 1個
register	動 登録する
beforehand	副 前もって
in turn	熟 順番に
display	名 ディスプレイ
preregistered	形 前もって登録された
enter	動 入力する
identification number	名 ID番号
conduct	動 行う
utilize	動 利用する
long-term	形 長期間の
absentee	名 欠席者
so that S 助動詞	接 Sが～するように
appropriate	形 適切な
free A from B	熟 AをBから解放する
chore	名 雑用
hand out	熟 配布する
affair	名 事務

▸単語10回CHECK 1 2 3 4 5 6 7 8 9 10

構文図解

[With the new system], the college expects 〈to cut some 425 hours of such burdensome work in the 1,700 lectures held in a year〉. [In the future], the school plans 〈to use the system for security-related matters〉. "Previously, it had been difficult for us to watch over our students in a comprehensive manner as no homeroom activities or similar sessions are available at universities," said Keiichiro Suzuki, deputy chief of the college. The system will help increase trust (from students and parents in the college) and prevent nuisance (related to checking attendance) [in case classes are formed according to the levels of students' proficiency].

M S V 不定詞 名詞的用法 O 過去分詞の後置修飾 M S V 不定詞 名詞的用法 O 形式主語のit 不定詞の主語と不定詞 名詞的用法 理由のas 同格のカンマ V S S′ S V O M increase ～と prevent ～の接続 V O 過去分詞の後置修飾 M M

本文訳

その新しいシステムで、大学は1年に実施される1,700の講義に付随する、そういった厄介な425時間の作業を削減できると期待する。将来、学校はセキュリティ関連の問題に、そのシステムを利用するつもりだ。「以前は、ホームルームやそれに似たような集まりが大学では利用できないので、私たちが*包括的な方法で学生を見守るのが難しかった」と、大学の副学長である鈴木敬一郎氏が言った。そのシステムがあると、大学に通う学生や保護者からの信頼を高めるのに役立つだろうし、学生の習熟度に応じて授業が行われる場合に、出席を確認することにかかわる面倒なことを防ぐことができるだろう。

*「包括的な」は、すべてをひっくるめているさまを意味する。

語彙リスト

burdensome	形	厄介な
lecture	名	講義
matter	名	問題
watch over	熟	見守る
comprehensive	形	包括的な
in a ～ manner	熟	～な方法で
session	名	集まり
deputy	名	副～
nuisance	名	面倒なこと
in case ～	熟	～の場合には
proficiency	名	習熟

▸単語10回CHECK 1 2 3 4 5 6 7 8 9 10

Facial recognition technology uses images captured by digital cameras to identify or confirm an individual's personal identity. It does this by checking the "biometric data" contained in those camera images against people's facial data (for example, size and shape of face, eye color, etc.) contained in government or commercial databases. Today, it is most commonly used in security systems to check people for access to secure places, computers, or computer networks. In many countries, it is also increasingly used by government agencies — especially by police and other law enforcement or public security agencies — for surveillance of people's movements and activities in public areas.

Hyogo College of Medicine has introduced a facial recognition technology-based system to check student attendance. It is the first university in Japan to use such a system, according to the institution in the city of Nishinomiya, Hyogo Prefecture. The university expects the system to allow teachers to check students' attendance swiftly and accurately and improve the work efficiency of its staff who, until recently, had been using standard attendance sheets.

Sixteen tablet devices with facial recognition functions were introduced on Friday last week, with four units — one for teachers and three for students — spread across four lecture rooms. The faces of a total of some 470 students had been registered on the devices beforehand. At the start of classes, students register their attendance using the tablets in turn. The devices are held up to their faces, and the images shown on the displays are checked against the preregistered images.

If the facial recognition functions do not work, students enter their identification numbers on the tablets for attendance registration. Teachers can check the attendance on their tablets, which show images of students conducting the facial recognition process in real time. The college also hopes to utilize the new system to identify long-term absentees at an early stage so that appropriate counseling will be provided to them.

The facial recognition system frees teachers from the chore of handing out attendance cards to students and collecting them, as well as entering attendance information into the college's educational affairs system. With the new system, the college expects to cut some 425 hours of such burdensome work in the 1,700 lectures held in a year. In the future, the school plans to use the system for security-related matters. "Previously, it had been difficult for us to watch over our students in a comprehensive manner as no homeroom activities or similar sessions are available at universities," said Keiichiro Suzuki, deputy chief of the college. The system will help increase trust from students and parents in the college and prevent nuisance related to checking attendance in case classes are formed according to the levels of students' proficiency.

▸音読10回CHECK 1 2 3 4 5 6 7 8 9 10

BACKGROUND KNOWLEDGE

生体認証

本問では**顔認証システム**が紹介されていますが、顔認証とは**生体認証**の1つです。**生体認証**とは、**網膜**、**指紋**、**掌**(てのひら)、**筆跡**、**声紋**、**顔**などのさまざまな身体的特徴を使った認識方法です。生体認証の特徴は、**従来の暗証番号等の認証にはつきものの"盗用"や"紛失"の危険性が低い点**です。

その中でも、**顔認証**とは、**目や鼻、口などの位置や大きさを基準に、本人かどうかを確認する認識方法**です。本問にもあったように、**データベースに保存されている本人画像とカメラが撮影した対象者の顔画像を照合し、認識**します。

顔認証の最大のメリットは、**多人数、広範囲という条件下でも認識が可能な点**です。本問で登場した**大学の学生の出欠管理**以外にも、**オフィスの入退管理システム**などでも利用されています。

顔認証システムは、上記のようなその人であることを証明する**個人の特定**といった用途がありますが、実はもう1つ、**マーケティングにおいて**も利用されています。

例えば、**表情やしぐさをもとに、顧客が今何を考えているか、ということに関する情報**が得られます。何らかのサービスを体験してもらい、その最中に**喜びの表情や満足げな表情が見られれば、そのサービスの質の高さを証明するもの**になるでしょう。

また、**紙のアンケートなどではうかがいしれない顧客の不満を掘り当てることも可能**になります。例えば、何らかのサービスの体験中に、**眉間にしわが寄る回数が多かったり、首をひねるような行為、あるいは下を向く回数が多ければ、顧客はそのサービスに不満を持っていると判断**することができます。

映画会社の中には、映画の試写会で、上映中に**顔認証システムを使用**して、**観客がいつ、どの場面で盛り上がるのか、そしていつ興味が失せてしまうのか**といったことの分析に活用している会社もあるそうです。

問題 4

健康

携帯機器の使用と睡眠

別冊p.14／制限時間25分／525 words

1. **その機器が近くにあるだけで、睡眠に影響が出る**

2. (a) ②　(b) ①　(c) ③

3. (d) ⑤　(e) ④

4. ③、④

5. **Some people have difficulty sleeping well. This may have something to do with the development of technology.**

1.

下線部(A)を日本語に訳しなさい。

構文図解

〈even having the presence of the device near you〉 affects sleep

(▲having：動名詞 have O C ／ 〈even … you〉：S ／ affects：V ／ sleep：O)

havingは**動名詞**でyouまでの名詞句を作り、文のSになる。Sの中身は、第5文型である**have O C「OをCにする」**が使われている。the presence of the deviceがO、near youがCで、「**その機器の存在を近くに置くこと**」＝「**その機器が近くにあること**」の意味。youは**一般総称**、すなわち**一般人を表すyou**なので日本語には訳さない。affectsがV、sleepがOの第3文型の文。まとめると、「**その機器が近くにあるだけで、睡眠に影響が出る**」が正解。

2.

空欄(a)～(c)を埋めるのに、最適な単語の数字を書きなさい。同じ単語を2度以上用いてはいけない。

① 活発な　② 継続的な　③ 不十分な

空欄(a)を含む文は、it's due to (a) stimulation from things like social media engagement「**それ（携帯を近くに置くだけで睡眠に影響が出ること）は、SNSとのつながりのようなものからの(a)な刺激が原因だ**」となる。すると、**一日を通じてSNSによって、継続的に刺激を受けるせいで、使っていなくても睡眠に影響が出る**とわかるので、(a)には② **continuous**が入るとわかる。

続いて、空欄(b)を含む文は、Your social group is (b) and you can be thinking about it「**あなたが所属する社会集団は(b)で、それについて常に考えている可能性がある**」となる。すると、**自分の関わる集団が活発なので、いつも考えている可能性がある**となるので、① **active**が空欄(b)に入るとわかる。

空欄(c)を含む文は、Bedtime device use was also tied to (c) sleep times of less than 10 hours per night for children「**就寝時間に機器を使用することは、子供には毎晩10時間未満の(c)睡眠時間にも結び付いていた**」となる。**子供にとって10時間に満たないこと**は、「**不十分な**」睡眠時間とわかるので、③ **insufficient**が入るとわかる。

3.

空欄(d)・(e)を埋めるのに、最適な単語の数字を書きなさい。同じ単語を2度以上用いてはいけない。

空欄(d)・(e)を含む文は、Two-thirds of teens leave a device (d) while sleeping in bed at night, and turning the device (e) or moving it to another room can make a big difference「**10代の若者の3分の2が、夜間寝ている間も携帯機器を(d)にしており、その機器の(e)、あるいは別の部屋に動かすことで、大きな変化をもたらす可能性がある**」になる。

すると、寝ている間も携帯の電源を**入れっぱなし**なので、**電源を切ること、**そして別の部屋に動かすことで、睡眠の結果に大きな影響を与える可能性があると推測できるので、**(d)には⑤ on**が、**(e)には④ off**が入るとわかる。⑤のonは**副詞のon**で、**leave ~ on**「**~の電源を入れっぱなしにする**」のように使用する。④は**turn ~ off**「**~の電源を切る**」の熟語。

4.

下の選択肢から2つの正しい文を選びなさい。

① もし子供や10代の若者たちが十分な睡眠をとりたいなら、夜の間、タブレットやスマートフォンの使用を避けるだけでよい。

② すべての機器が、一定の時間で自動的に電源が落ちるので、子供や10代の若者はマイナスの影響から守られるだろう。

③ 人が夜間に目覚めて、電話がベッドの近くにあると、たいていメールを読み、それが睡眠に影響する。

④ 人は睡眠の重要性を見過ごす傾向にあり、結果として、健康上の問題に苦しむ。

⑤ 機器の使用は有益だから、私たちはその有害な側面について心配する必要はない。

正解の選択肢から見ていくと、③は**第9段落第1文 "It's normal to wake up during the night but when the phone is there, many people instead of just turning over will tap on the phone ostensibly to check the time, will see 15 text messages from their buddy or whatever「夜間目覚めるのは通常のことだが、電話がそこにあると、単に寝返りをするかわりに、多くの人が、表向きは時間を調べるのに電話に触れて、そして仲間からの15通のメールやら何やらを見るだろう**」と一致するので正解。

④は**最終段落第1文、第2文Poor sleep has been tied to many health outcomes ~. "Sleep is an exposure that we take for granted, is free and we don't take enough notice of it."**「**睡眠不足は、多くの健康上の結果に結びついてきたと~。"睡眠は、無料だと当たり前に思う体験であり、私たちはそれに十分な注意を払っていない"**」と一致するので、正解。クォーテーションマーク(" ")内のSleep ~ freeまでの文構造が難しいので、説明する。

構文 POINT ❹ 連鎖関係詞

（例文）

He is the man **who I thought was your father**.

訳 彼はあなたの父親だと私が思った人だ。

連鎖関係詞は、**関係詞の後ろにSVVの並びがくることが多い**のが特徴です。例文でもwhoの後ろにI thought wasとSVVの並びが現れています。この並びを見たら**連鎖関係詞**と特定して、後ろから順に訳して、「あなたの父親だと私が思った人」とします。

本文に戻ると、**Sleep is an exposure that we take for granted, is free**は、thatの後ろで**we take for grantedがSV、isがVなのでSVVの並びから、thatを連鎖関係詞**と特定する。後ろから訳して、「**無料だと私たちが当たり前に思う体験**」となる。

残りの不正解の選択肢を見ていくと、①は**第11段落第1文Two-thirds of teens leave a device on while sleeping in bed at night, and turning the device off or moving it to another room can make a big difference, ～.「10代の若者の3分の2が、夜間寝ている間も携帯機器の電源をつけっぱなしにしており、その機器の電源を切る、あるいは別の部屋に動かすことで、大きな変化をもたらす可能性がある**」から、**使用を避けるだけではなく、電源を切る、あるいは別の部屋に動かすことが必要なので、不適。**

②は**第13段落第1文Some devices can be programmed to switch off at a certain hour「携帯機器の中には、一定の時間に電源が切れる設定が可能なものもある**」とあるだけで、all devicesと書いていないので不適。

解法 POINT ❸ 言い過ぎの選択肢に注意

誤りの選択肢は、**100%ワードを使った“言い過ぎ”の内容になっている**ことがよくあります。**always「いつも」**、**necessarily「必ず」**、**all「すべて」**、**every「すべての」**といった表現です。本文ではそこまで言っていないのに、**選択肢で言い過ぎる**ことで、誤りの選択肢を作ります。上記の表現を見たら、「**本当にそこまで言っていたか？**」をチェックするようにしましょう。

⑤は**第12段落第2文 we need to recognize that there are negative consequences of some device use「携帯機器の使い方によっては、マイナスの影響もあると私たちは認識する必要がある」**に反するので不適。

5.

次の日本語の下線部を英語に直しなさい。この文章の表現を使ってもよい。

<u>よく眠るのが難しい人もいる</u>。<u>これには科学技術の発展が関係あるのかもしれない</u>。科学技術は我々の生活をより快適にするはずなのだが。

第1文は「**～する人もいる**」から、**Some people ～ .**を使う。「**よく眠るのが難しい**」は「**しっかりと眠るのが難しい**」と変換できるので、**have difficulty sleeping well**で表す。第1文は**Some people have difficulty sleeping well.**となる。**have difficulty doing**「**～するのが難しい**」に注意する。

第2文は**have something to do with**「**～と関係がある**」を使って、**This may have something to do with the development of technology**.で表す。

構文図解

Health News

November 1, 2016

〈Using, and even just thinking about portable media〉 may disrupt kids' sleep

動名詞 S 動名詞 V O

Children and teens (with access to tablets and smartphones at night) don't get enough sleep and are sleepier [during the day], [whether or not they use the devices], [according to a new review].

S M V O V C M M M Children and teensを指す

The review (of 20 previous studies) found 〈kids using portable media devices around bedtime were more than twice as likely as kids who didn't use them to have short sleep times, but so were kids who had access to such devices at night but didn't use them〉.

S M V 名詞節のthatの省略 現在分詞の後置修飾 O twice as ～ as...「…の2倍～」 portable media devicesを指す be likely to doのto do 倒置 関係代名詞 portable media devicesを指す

"A lot of people argue that it's the device light emission that leads to sleep outcomes, but even if you're not using it, even having the presence of the device near you affects sleep," said lead author Ben Carter (of King's College London).

O 名詞節のthat 強調構文 (It is A that ～.) the deviceを指す 動名詞 have O C V S M

"My personal view is it's due to continuous stimulation from things like social media engagement," and that there may be a similar relationship with adults, Carter told Reuters Health.

名詞節のthatの省略 O_2 枕元に携帯があると睡眠に影響すること 前置詞のlike it's ～ engagementとthat ～ adultsの接続 名詞節のthat S V O_1

本文訳

ヘルス・ニュース
2016年11月1日
携帯機器を使うことやそれについて考えるだけでも、子供の睡眠を妨げるかもしれない

新しい報告によると、夜にタブレットやスマートフォンを利用できる子供や10代の若者は、その機器を使っても使わなくても、十分な睡眠をとれなかったり、日中により眠くなったりするという。

以前に行われた20の研究に関する報告でわかったことは、就寝時間の前後で携帯メディア機器を使う子供は、それらを使わない子供より睡眠時間が短くなる可能性が2倍以上あるが、夜間にそういった機器を利用できるが、使わない子供もそうなる可能性が2倍以上あるということだ。

「たくさんの人が、睡眠の結果に影響するのは、その機器の光の放出によるものだと主張するが、たとえそれを使っていなくても、近くにその機器があるだけで、睡眠に影響を与える」と、キングス・カレッジ・ロンドンの筆頭著者であるベン・カーターは言った。

「私の個人的な見解は、SNSとのつながりのようなものから継続的に受ける刺激が原因」であって、大人でも同様の関連があるかもしれない、とカーターはロイター・ヘルス・ニュースに伝えた。

語彙リスト

□	portable	形 携帯できる
□	disrupt	動 乱す
□	access to	熟 ～を利用する機会
□	device	名 機器
□	review	名 再調査
□	previous	形 以前の
□	be likely to do	熟 ～する可能性がある
□	argue	動 主張する
□	light	名 光
□	emission	名 放出
□	lead to	熟 ～につながる
□	outcome	名 結果
□	even if	接 たとえ～でも
□	presence	名 存在
□	affect	動 影響する
□	lead author	名 筆頭著者
□	due to	熟 ～が原因で
□	continuous	形 継続的な
□	stimulation	名 刺激
□	engagement	名 つながり
□	similar	形 同様の
□	relationship	名 関連

▸単語10回CHECK 1 □ 2 □ 3 □ 4 □ 5 □ 6 □ 7 □ 8 □ 9 □ 10 □

構文図解

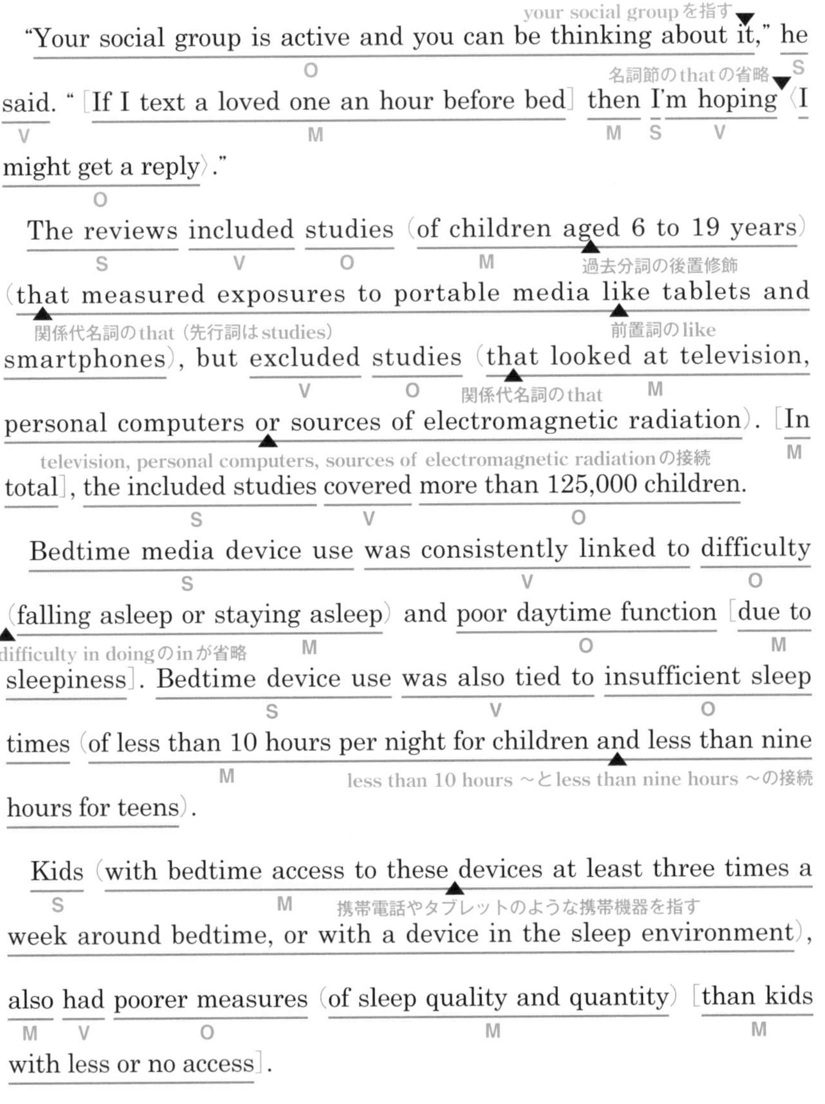

"Your social group is active and you can be thinking about it," he said. "[If I text a loved one an hour before bed] then I'm hoping 〈I might get a reply〉."
The reviews included studies (of children aged 6 to 19 years) (that measured exposures to portable media like tablets and smartphones), but excluded studies (that looked at television, personal computers or sources of electromagnetic radiation). [In total], the included studies covered more than 125,000 children.
Bedtime media device use was consistently linked to difficulty (falling asleep or staying asleep) and poor daytime function [due to sleepiness]. Bedtime device use was also tied to insufficient sleep times (of less than 10 hours per night for children and less than nine hours for teens).
Kids (with bedtime access to these devices at least three times a week around bedtime, or with a device in the sleep environment), also had poorer measures (of sleep quality and quantity) [than kids with less or no access].
your social group を指す
名詞節の that の省略
過去分詞の後置修飾
関係代名詞の that（先行詞は studies）
前置詞の like
関係代名詞の that
television, personal computers, sources of electromagnetic radiation の接続
difficulty in doing の in が省略
less than 10 hours ～と less than nine hours ～の接続
携帯電話やタブレットのような携帯機器を指す

本文訳

「あなたが所属する社会集団は活発で、それについて常に考えている可能性がある」と彼は言った。「もし私が、寝る1時間前に愛する人にメールを送るなら、返信がくるかもしれないと期待してしまう」。

その批評には、タブレットやスマートフォンのような携帯メディアにどれほどさらされているかを計測した、6歳～19歳の子供の研究を含めているが、テレビ、パソコン、電磁放射線の源にさらされているかを調べる研究は除外した。合計で、その研究では、12万5千人以上の子供を対象とした。

就寝時間にメディア機器を使用することは、熟睡や睡眠の継続の難しさや、眠気が原因で日中の機能が低下することに絶えず結び付いていた。就寝前の機器の使用は、子供には毎晩10時間未満、そして10代の若者には9時間未満の不十分な睡眠時間にも結び付いていた。

就寝時間周辺に、これらの機器を、少なくとも週に3回使用する、あるいは睡眠環境にその機器がある子供も、より少ない頻度やまったく携帯機器を利用しない子供より睡眠の質や量が低く計測された。

語彙リスト

□	text	動 携帯でメールを送る
□	loved one	名 最愛の人
□	reply	名 返信
□	include	動 含んでいる
□	aged ~	形 ~歳の
□	measure	動 計測する
□	exposure to	熟 ~にさらされること
□	exclude	動 除外する
□	look at	熟 ~を調べる
□	source	名 源
□	electromagnetic	形 電磁気の
□	radiation	名 放射線
□	in total	熟 合計で
□	cover	動 対象とする
□	consistently	副 絶えず
□	be linked to	熟 ~に関係している
□	fall asleep	熟 ぐっすり眠る
□	function	名 機能
□	be tied to	熟 ~に結び付けられる
□	quality	名 質
□	quantity	名 量

▶単語10回CHECK 1 □ 2 □ 3 □ 4 □ 5 □ 6 □ 7 □ 8 □ 9 □ 10 □

構文図解

"It's normal to wake up during the night but when the phone is there, many people instead of just turning over will tap on the phone ostensibly to check the time, will see 15 text messages from their buddy or whatever, then 2 hours later they're going back to bed," said Dr. Charles Czeisler 〈at Brigham and Women's Hospital in Boston〉.

形式主語 / 不定詞 名詞的用法 / turning overとtap on the phoneの対比 / 不定詞 副詞的用法 / many peopleがS / O / many peopleを指す / V / S / M

"It's very engaging technology and when it's present in the bedroom it reduces sleep duration," said Czeisler, who coauthored an editorial [alongside the review].

携帯機器を指す / 携帯機器を指す / 携帯機器を指す / O / V / S / V / O / M

Two-thirds of teens leave a device on while sleeping in bed at night, and turning the device off or moving it to another room can make a big difference, he told Reuters Health.

O_2 / they (= teens) areの省略 / the deviceを指す / S / V / O_1

"Device use is ubiquitous and they are hugely beneficial in some cases," Carter said. "However, we need to recognize 〈that there are negative consequences of some device use〉."

O / 携帯機器を指す / S / V / M / S / V / 名詞節のthat / O

Some devices can be programmed to switch off at a certain hour, which Carter would strongly encourage, he said.

不定詞 副詞的用法 / O / S / V

本文訳

「夜間目覚めるのは通常のことだが、電話がそこにあると、単に寝返りをするかわりに、多くの人が、表向きは時間を調べるのに電話に触れて、そして仲間からの15通のメールやら何やらを見て、2時間後に眠りに戻るだろう」と、ボストンのブリガム・アンド・ウィミンズ病院のチャールズ・ツァイスラーは言った。

「それはとても魅力的なテクノロジーで、寝室にあると、睡眠の継続時間を減らす」と、その報告に沿って*社説を共著したツァイスラーは言った。

10代の若者の3分の2が、夜間寝ている間も携帯機器の電源をつけっぱなしにしており、その機器の電源を切る、あるいは別の部屋に動かすことで、大きな変化をもたらす可能性があると彼はロイター・ヘルス・ニュースに伝えた。

「機器の使用はどこでもできることで、場合によってはとても有益になる」とカーターは言った。「しかし、使い方によっては、マイナスの影響もあると私たちは認識する必要がある」。

携帯機器の中には、一定の時間に電源が切れる設定が可能なものもあり、そうすることをカーターは強く推奨していると彼は言った。

*「社説」は、新聞などでその社の主張として掲載する論説のこと。

語彙リスト

□	instead of	熟 ～の代わりに
□	turn over	熟 寝返りする
□	tap on	熟 軽くたたく
□	ostensibly	副 表向きには
□	buddy	名 仲間
□	～ or whatever	熟 ～かそのようなもの
□	engaging	形 魅力的な
□	present	形 存在して
□	duration	名 持続時間
□	coauthor	動 共著する
□	editorial	名 社説
□	alongside	前 ～に沿って
□	leave ～ on	熟 ～をつけっぱなしにする
□	make a difference	熟 違いを作る
□	ubiquitous	形 どこにでもある
□	hugely	副 膨大に
□	beneficial	形 役に立つ
□	consequence	名 影響
□	be programmed to do	熟 ～するように設定されている
□	switch off	熟 電源が切れる
□	certain	形 一定の

▸単語10回CHECK 1 □ 2 □ 3 □ 4 □ 5 □ 6 □ 7 □ 8 □ 9 □ 10 □

構文図解

many health outcomesを指す

Poor sleep has been tied to many health outcomes, among them dementia, Carter said. "Sleep is an exposure (that we take for granted, is free) and we don't take enough notice of it."

O S V S V C M S V O

連鎖関係詞「無料だと当たり前に思う」

sleepを指す

本文訳

睡眠不足は、*認知症を含めた多くの健康上の結果に結び付いてきたとカーターは言った。「睡眠は、無料だと当たり前に思う体験であり、私たちはそれに十分に注意を払っていない」。

*「認知症」は、脳の病気や脳に損傷を受けることなどにより認知機能が低下する状態のこと。

語彙リスト

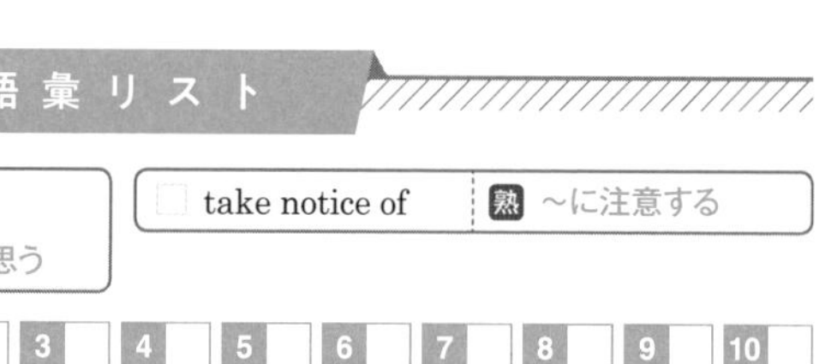

dementia	名	認知症
take O for granted	熟	Oを当然と思う
take notice of	熟	～に注意する

▶ 単語10回CHECK 1 2 3 4 5 6 7 8 9 10

Health News
November 1, 2016

Using, and even just thinking about portable media may disrupt kids' sleep

Children and teens with access to tablets and smartphones at night don't get enough sleep and are sleepier during the day, whether or not they use the devices, according to a new review.

The review of 20 previous studies found kids using portable media devices around bedtime were more than twice as likely as kids who didn't use them to have short sleep times, but so were kids who had access to such devices at night but didn't use them.

"A lot of people argue that it's the device light emission that leads to sleep outcomes, but even if you're not using it, even having the presence of the device near you affects sleep," said lead author Ben Carter of King's College London.

"My personal view is it's due to continuous stimulation from things like social media engagement," and that there may be a similar relationship with adults, Carter told Reuters Health.

"Your social group is active and you can be thinking about it," he said. "If I text a loved one an hour before bed then I'm hoping I might get a reply."

The reviews included studies of children aged 6 to 19 years that measured exposures to portable media like tablets and smartphones, but excluded studies that looked at television, personal computers or sources of electromagnetic radiation. In total, the included studies covered more than 125,000 children.

Bedtime media device use was consistently linked to difficulty falling asleep or staying asleep and poor daytime function due to sleepiness. Bedtime device use was also tied to insufficient sleep times of less than 10 hours per night for children and less than nine hours for teens.

Kids with bedtime access to these devices at least three times a week around bedtime, or with a device in the sleep environment, also had poorer measures of sleep quality and quantity than kids with less or no access.

"It's normal to wake up during the night but when the phone is there, many people instead of just turning over will tap on the phone ostensibly to check the time, will see 15 text messages from their buddy or whatever, then 2 hours later they're going back to bed," said Dr. Charles Czeisler at Brigham and Women's Hospital in Boston.

"It's very engaging technology and when it's present in the bedroom it reduces sleep duration," said Czeisler, who coauthored an editorial alongside the review.

Two-thirds of teens leave a device on while sleeping in bed at night, and turning the device off or moving it to another room can make a big difference, he told Reuters Health.

"Device use is ubiquitous and they are hugely beneficial in some cases," Carter said. "However, we need to recognize that there are negative consequences of some device use."

Some devices can be programmed to switch off at a certain hour, which Carter would strongly encourage, he said.

Poor sleep has been tied to many health outcomes, among them dementia, Carter said. "Sleep is an exposure that we take for granted, is free and we don't take enough notice of it."

▸音読10回CHECK 1 2 3 4 5 6 7 8 9 10

BACKGROUND KNOWLEDGE

スマホ脳

前作『**大学入試　レベル別英語長文問題　ソリューション1　スタンダードレベル**』の第9問のコラムで、**携帯依存症**について説明しました。携帯機器は、上手に使えばとても便利なものですが、依存症も含めてさまざまな問題を抱えているので、現代の専門家から批評される代物でもあります。

とりわけ、青少年への影響は甚大（じんだい）なものでしょう。スティーブ・ジョブズ氏は、自らが作ったiPadを、自分の子供には、その使用時間を厳しく制限していました。また、ビル・ゲイツ氏は子供が14歳になるまでスマホを持たせなかったようです。これは、前述したように、**スマホやタブレットへの依存が学習の基となる集中力、忍耐力に悪影響を与える**ことを、その発明者自身が認識していたからに他なりません。

スウェーデンの精神科医であるアンデシュ・ハンセン氏による『**スマホ脳**』という本が、世界的ベストセラーになりました。著者によると、携帯依存症の原因は、携帯電話を使って新しい知識に触れることで、**脳にドーパミンという快楽物質が放出される『報酬系』の仕組みに関係**しているようです。

本問にあったように、携帯電話を傍（かたわ）らに置くだけで、学習効果、記憶力、集中力は低下するそうです。**何かをしながら携帯電話をいじるようないわゆるマルチタスクが、記憶力、集中力の低下を引き起こす**そうです。私たちができる唯一の抵抗手段は、**必要な時以外は携帯電話を持ち歩かない、電源を入れない**こと、つまり**携帯電話を遠ざける時間を作ること**でしょう。

私自身も、この本ですすめられていたように、**寝室に携帯電話を持ち込まない**ようになってから**驚くほど睡眠の質が高まって、日中の集中力や気分の安定**がもたらされています。みなさんも、ぜひ**寝室から携帯電話を遠ざけてみて**ください。

問題
5

IT・テクノロジー

AIがもたらす変化

別冊p.18／制限時間25分／575 words

解答

(1) エ

(2) 雇用者となりうる人が、オンライン上の仕事の経歴やソーシャルメディアの映像を含んだ、さまざまなデータソースから情報を引き出して、人やその技術を見つけるから。

(3) イ

(4) そうしたシステムを設計する人が意図的だろうとそうでなかろうと、そのシステムを彼らの偏見で満たしてしまう危険性。

(5) 自分たちの生活をよくするのに、これらのテクノロジーを応用する方法を理解すること。

(6) ウ

解説

(1)

下線部(1) **not unlike the way email tries to finish spelling a word for users today**はnotとunlike「～と違って」から**二重否定**なので、強い肯定の意味になり「**～とよく似た**」となる。

語彙 POINT ❹ 二重否定

二重否定の表現は、通常の肯定表現より意味が強くなることに注意します。以下に代表的な二重否定の表現をまとめます。
not unlike「～とよく似た」／ never fail to do「必ず～する」
cannot A without B「BなしでAできない」＝「Aすると必ずBする」

続いて、**the way SV「SがVする方法」**から、まとめると「**現在、メールが単語のスペリングを完成させてくれるのとよく似た方法で**」となるので、**(エ)** が正解とわかる。

(2)

下線部(2)の後ろの文が理由を表すと判断して、そこをまとめる。**Potential employers will draw from different data sources, including online business profiles and social media streams, to find out about a person and their skills.**「**雇用者となりうる人が、オンライン上の仕事の経歴やソーシャルメディアの映像を含んだ、さまざまなデータソースから情報を引き出して、人やその技術を見つけるから**」が正解。

including「**～を含んで**」から**前置詞句**が始まり、streamsまでの意味のカタマリを作り、**different data sourcesの具体例**になっている。to findは**不定詞の副詞的用法**で「**結果**」の意味になることに注意する。

(3)

(ア) さらなる　(イ) より少ない　(ウ) 古風な　(エ) 個人的な

空欄(A)を含む文は、**In theory, this kind of online job matching could lead to (A) bias and discrimination in hiring practices.** となる。**面接で直接の接点をとるよりも、オンライン上の客観的な情報のほうが、一般的に偏見や差別は減る**ので、**(イ) less** が正解となる。

論理 POINT ❶ 理論⇒逆接⇒実際の流れ

空欄(A)を含む文で、**In theory**「**理論上**」とあり、その後ろの文のHoweverから「**実際**」のことが述べられ、対比構造になっていることに気づきましょう。頻出の対比構造をまとめます。
国の対比(日本とアメリカなど) / **時の対比**(昔と今の対比)
男女の対比 / **一般論と筆者の主張の対比** / **理想と現実の対比**

(4)

論理 POINT ② there be 構文のSは抽象の目印

There be 構文のSは抽象表現の目印になるので、**後ろの文からその具体例が続きます。** There be 構文とその後ろの文の間に「**例えば**」や「**すなわち**」と日本語を補って、見えない文のつながりを見抜きましょう。

本問でも、下線部(3)の**potential pitfalls**「**思わぬ危険**」が**抽象表現**で、その後ろの文から**具体説明**が続くので、「**すなわち**」と補って文と文のつながりを見抜く。**the people who are building these tools aren't informing these tools with their own biases, whether they're intentional or not**から「**そうしたシステムを設計する人が意図的だろうとそうでなかろうと、そのシステムを彼らの偏見で満たしてしまう危険性**」が正解。**inform A with B**「**AをBで満たす**」に注意する。

(5)

下線部(4)を含む文は、**it is critical for the public to get engaged now, rather than sitting back and letting technology happen to them**「**大衆が手をこまねいて、テクノロジーが自分の身に降りかかってくるままでいるよりむしろ、今積極的にかかわることがとても重要だ**」となる。問題文で「具体的に」という指示があるので、**最終段落の最終文**で、下線部(4)が具体化されているので、ここをまとめる。

下線部と波線部の対応関係に注目する。we're just kind of sitting back and letting technology tell us what jobs we'll have and what jobs we won't have, rather than **us figuring out how to apply these technologies to improve our lives**「**私たちが生活をよくするのにこれらのテクノロジーを応用する方法を理解する**よりむしろ、ただ手をこまねいて、テクノロジーに、私たちがどんな仕事に就けるか、どんな仕事に就けないかを告げてもらう」となる。**下線部(4)が理想**であるのに対して、**この文は手前のa deep concernから深い懸念**なので、B rather than AのBとAが逆になっていることを理解する。よって、「**自分たちの生活をよくするのにこれらのテクノロジーを応用する方法を理解すること**」が正解となる。

(6)

（ア）人工知能は私たちに代わって、すべての仕事を行うだろう。
（イ）私たちはみんな、オンラインで仕事を探すだろう。
（ウ）私たちの働き方は、近い将来著しく変わるだろう。
（エ）私たちは仕事をする際に、テクノロジーを援助するだろう。

（ウ）は、**第1段落第1文、同段落最終文、第2段落第1文**などからも十分に読み取れる内容なので、正解となる。

不正解の選択肢を見ていくと、（ア）は、**第2段落第2文** By 2030, we'll likely be living in a world where artificial assistants help us with **almost every task**「2030年までに、私たちはおそらく、人工知能の助手が**ほとんどすべての仕事**を手伝ってくれる世界で暮らすことになるだろう」とあるだけで、**すべての仕事を行うとは書かれていないので不適。**p.59の 解法 POINT ❸ で見たように、**言い過ぎの選択肢に注意**する。（エ）も、この文とは反対の内容なので不適。

（イ）も、**第4段落にオンライン上の仕事のマッチングシステムの可能性が書かれている**が、**みんながオンライン上で仕事を探すとは書かれていない**ので不適。これも、**言い過ぎの選択肢**である。

構文図解

Up to 85 percent (of the jobs) (that today's college students will have in 11 years) haven't been invented yet. That's [according to a panel of experts assembled by the Institute for the Future], [although an exact percentage is impossible to predict]. The IFTF, an organization that seeks to identify emerging trends and their impacts on global society, forecasts ⟨that many of the tasks and duties of the jobs that today's young people will hold in 2030 don't exist right now⟩.

S: Up to 85 percent / M: (of the jobs) / M: (that today's college students will have in 11 years) / V: haven't been invented / M: yet / S: That / V: 's / M: [according to a panel of experts assembled by the Institute for the Future] / M: [although an exact percentage is impossible to predict] / S: The IFTF / S′: an organization that seeks to identify emerging trends and their impacts on global society / V: forecasts / O: ⟨that many of the tasks and duties of the jobs that today's young people will hold in 2030 don't exist right now⟩

関係代名詞のthat
今の大学生が11年後に就く仕事のうち、85%までがまだないこと
時の経過のin「〜後に」
過去分詞の名詞修飾
不定詞　副詞的用法　形容詞修飾
同格のカンマ
関係代名詞のthat
名詞節のthat
関係代名詞のthat（that〜2030までの形容詞節）

"Those who plan to work for the next 50 years have to have a mindset of, 'I'm going to be working and learning and working and learning, and working and learning,' in order to make a career," says Rachel Maguire, a research director with IFTF. [By 2030], we'll likely be living [in a world where artificial assistants help us with almost every task, not unlike the way email tries to finish spelling a word for users today]. Maguire says ⟨it will be like having an assistant working alongside you, taking on tasks at which the human brain does not excel⟩.

O: "Those who plan to work ... in order to make a career," / V: says / S: Rachel Maguire / S′: a research director with IFTF / M: [By 2030] / S: we / V: 'll likely be living / M: [in a world where ... for users today] / S: Maguire / V: says / O: ⟨it will be like having an assistant working alongside you, taking on tasks at which the human brain does not excel⟩

Those who「〜する人々」（who〜yearsまでの形容詞節）
同格のカンマ「すなわち」
関係副詞
the way SV「SがVする方法」
名詞節のthatの省略
前置詞のlike
人工知能が助けてくれる世界
have O doing「Oをさせる」のdoing
have O doingのdoingの並列

The U.S. Bureau (of Labor Statistics) says ⟨today's students will have eight to 10 jobs by the time they are 38⟩.

S: The U.S. Bureau / M: (of Labor Statistics) / V: says / O: ⟨today's students will have eight to 10 jobs by the time they are 38⟩

名詞節のthatの省略
today's studentsを指す

本文訳

今日の大学生が11年後に就くであろう仕事のうち、85％までがまだ作られていない。それは、正確なパーセンテージは予測できないけれども、未来研究所が集めた専門家委員会による見解だ。国際社会への新しい傾向や影響を見極めようとする組織であるIFTF（未来研究所）は、今日の若者が2030年に行うであろう仕事の作業や任務の多くが、今は存在していないと予測する。

「次の50年を働く予定の人は、『キャリアを形成するのに、働いて学んで働いて学んで働いて学ぶつもりだ』という考え方でいなければならない」と、IFTFの研究所の所長であるレイチェル・マグワイアは言う。2030年までに、現在、メールが単語のスペリングを完成させてくれるのとよく似た方法で、私たちはおそらく、人工知能の助手が、私たちのほとんどすべての仕事を手伝ってくれる世界で暮らすことになるだろう。マグワイアは、それは、助手をあなたのそばで働かせて、人間の脳では追い付かない作業をさせるようなものだろうと言う。

アメリカ合衆国労働統計局は、今日の学生は38歳になるまでに、8～10の仕事をするようになるだろうと言う。

語彙リスト

up to	熟	～まで
panel	名	委員会
assemble	動	集める
institute	名	研究所
exact	形	正確な
predict	動	予測する
organization	名	組織
seek to do	熟	～しようとする
identify	動	確認する
emerging	形	新興の
trend	名	傾向
impact	名	影響
global	形	世界的な
task	名	作業
duty	名	義務
mindset	名	考え方
director	名	所長
likely	副	たぶん～だろう
artificial	形	人工の
assistant	名	助手
help A with B	熟	AのBを手伝う
spell	動	～をつづる
alongside	前	～のそばで
take on	熟	～を引き受ける
excel	動	秀でる
bureau	名	局
statistics	名	統計
by the time ～	接	～する時までには

▶単語10回CHECK 1 2 3 4 5 6 7 8 9 10

1 健康 2 心理 3 IT・テクノロジー 4 健康 5 IT・テクノロジー 6 IT・テクノロジー 7 環境 8 文化 9 環境 10 社会

構 文 図 解

today's studentsを指す
And they won't necessarily have to take time away [from any one of
S V O M M
those jobs for training] or to gain additional qualifications (related to
to take ～とto gain ～の接続 V O 過去分詞の後置修飾
their fields). Instead, they'll partner [with machines] [for on-the-job
M M S V M M
learning], [wearing an augmented reality headset that will give
分詞構文 today's students M 関係代名詞のthat
them the information they need in real-time to get the work done]. "It
today's studentsを指す 関係詞の省略 不定詞 副詞的用法 機械と手を組むこと
eliminates the need for people to leave a job in order to learn a new
O peopleを指す 不定詞の主語 不定詞 形容詞的用法 機械と手を組むこと
skill so they can level up and earn more money," Maguire says. "It
so that S 助動詞 のthatが省略 S V S
gives the opportunity (for people to be able to learn those kinds of
V O 不定詞の主語 不定詞 形容詞的用法 (the opportunityを修飾)
new skills and demonstrate proficiency in-the-moment at the job)."
M learn ～とdemonstrate ～の接続

And forget [about traditional human resources departments or the
V M
challenging task of looking for a job on your own]. [In the future],
M
the job might come [to you]. Potential employers will draw [from
S V M S V M
different data sources, including online business profiles and social
「～を含んで」
media streams], [to find out about a person and their skills].
不定詞 副詞的用法 M
Maguire says 〈there's already a lot of activity around turning
S V 名詞節のthatの省略 O
employment into a matchmaking endeavor, using artificial
turn A into B「AをBに変える」のinto 分詞構文
intelligence and deep learning to help the right person and the right
不定詞 副詞的用法
job find each other〉.
help O doのdo

本文訳

そして、彼らは必ずしも研修のためにそうした仕事の1つから離れて時間を取ったり、あるいはその分野に関する追加の資格を取得しなくてもよいだろう。その代わりに、その仕事をするのにすぐに必要な情報を提供してくれる*拡張現実ヘッドセットを身に着けて、仕事をしながら学習するため、機械と手を組むだろう。「それは、人がレベルアップする、あるいはもっとお金を稼ごうと、新しい技術を身に付けるために仕事を離れる必要性をなくすものだ」とマグワイアは言う。「それは、人がそうした種類の新しい技術を身に付けて、一瞬で仕事の習熟度を示すことができる機会を与えてくれる」。

そして、従来の人事部や自分で仕事を探すという骨の折れる作業を忘れなさい。将来、仕事が、あなたのもとにやってくるかもしれない。雇用者となりうる人が、人やその人の技術を見つけるのに、オンライン上の仕事の経歴やソーシャルメディアの映像を含んだ、さまざまな*データソースから情報を引き出すだろう。マグワイアは、適材適所の配置を手助けするために、人工知能や*ディープラーニングを使って、雇用を仲介へと変える動きが、すでにたくさん存在すると言う。

* 「拡張現実」は、現実世界に3Dデータ、動画などで情報を加え、現実の情報を実体よりも強調して伝える技術のこと。
* 「データソース」は、あるシステムが利用するデータの保管場所のこと。
* 「ディープラーニング」は、深層学習のことで、コンピューターによる機械学習で、従来より深い階層のネットワークにより、人間の力なしに機械が自動的にデータから特徴を抽出する学習のこと。

語彙リスト

not necessarily	熟	必ずしも～な訳ではない
take time	熟	時間をとる
additional	形	追加の
qualification	名	資格
be related to	熟	～に関係している
field	名	分野
partner with	熟	～と組む
on-the-job	形	仕事中の
augmented reality	名	拡張現実
eliminate	動	削除する
demonstrate	動	示す
proficiency	名	熟練
moment	名	瞬間
human resources	名	人事
department	名	部署
challenging	形	骨の折れる
on one's own	熟	自分自身で
potential	形	潜在的な
employer	名	雇用者
draw	動	引き出す
including	前	～を含んで
stream	名	ストリーミング
matchmaking	名	仲介
endeavor	名	試み
artificial intelligence	名	人工知能

▶単語10回CHECK 1 2 3 4 5 6 7 8 9 10

構文図解

In theory, 〈this kind of〉 online job matching could lead to less bias and discrimination 〈in hiring practices〉. However, there are potential pitfalls. "We have to make sure that the people who are building these tools aren't informing these tools with their own biases, whether they're intentional or not," Maguire says. "These systems will only be as good [as the data that feeds them]."

Which leads Maguire [to another point]. [While she doesn't want to sound melodramatic about emerging technologies], she believes 〈it is critical for the public to get engaged now, rather than sitting back and letting technology happen to them〉. "What do we want from these new technological capabilities, and how do we make sure we put in place the social policies and systems that will result in what it is we all want?" she says. "I have a deep concern 〈that we're just kind of sitting back and letting technology tell us what jobs we'll have and what jobs we won't have, rather than us figuring out how to apply these technologies to improve our lives〉."

M / M / S / V / O（In theory, / this kind of / online job matching / could lead to / less bias and discrimination）
M（in hiring practices）/ M（However）/ M（there）/ V（are）/ S（potential pitfalls）
O（"We have to make sure ...）
名詞節のthat
online job matchingを指す
online job matchingを指す
the peopleを指す
S（These systems）/ V（will only be）/ C（as good）/ M（as the data ...）
関係代名詞 先行詞は前文
関係代名詞のthat
these systemsを指す
S（Which）/ V（leads）/ O（Maguire）/ M（to another point）/ M（While ...）
S（she）/ V（believes）
形式主語
名詞節のthatの省略 O
不定詞の主語
不定詞 名詞的用法
online job matchingなどのAIを用いた技術
the publicを指す
O（"What do we want ...）
名詞節のthatの省略
強調構文（it is that ～.）のthatが省略された間接疑問文
関係代名詞のthat
S（she）/ V（says）/ S（I）/ V（have）/ O（a deep concern）
同格のthat
M
「どんな名詞を～か」
B rather than A「AというよりむしろB」
不定詞 副詞的用法

本文訳

理論上は、この種のオンライン上の仕事の仲介システムは、雇用の慣例で見られた偏見や差別を減らす可能性がある。しかし、思わぬ危険がある。「私たちはそうしたシステムを設計する人が意図的だろうとそうでなかろうと、そのシステムを彼らの偏見で満たしていないように注意しなければならない」とマグワイアは言う。「これらのシステムは、単に入力するデータの質次第になるだろう」。

そのことで、マグワイアはもう1つの重要な点に気付く。彼女は新しいテクノロジーに浮かれているようには思われたくないが、大衆が手をこまねいて、テクノロジーが自分の身に降りかかってくるままでいるよりむしろ、今積極的にかかわることがとても重要だと信じている。「私たちはこうした新しいテクノロジーの力から何を欲するのか、そして私たち全員が望むものを生み出す社会政策や制度をどうやって確実に配備するか」と彼女は言う。「私たちが生活をよくするのにこれらのテクノロジーを応用する方法を理解するよりむしろ、ただ手をこまねいていて、テクノロジーに、私たちがどんな仕事に就けるか、どんな仕事に就けないかを告げてもらうことに深い懸念を抱いている」。

語彙リスト

語句	品詞	意味
in theory	熟	理論上
lead to	熟	～につながる
bias	名	偏見
discrimination	名	差別
practice	名	慣例
pitfall	名	危険
make sure	熟	注意する
inform A with B	熟	AをBで満たす
intentional	形	意図的な
feed	動	供給する
melodramatic	形	メロドラマ的な
critical	形	決定的な
the public	熟	大衆
get engaged	熟	かかわる
sit back	熟	(何もせずに)傍観(ぼうかん)する
capability	名	能力
result in	熟	～という結果になる
concern	名	懸念
figure out	熟	理解する
apply O to do	熟	Oを～するように応用する

▶単語10回CHECK 1 2 3 4 5 6 7 8 9 10

Up to 85 percent of the jobs that today's college students will have in 11 years haven't been invented yet. That's according to a panel of experts assembled by the Institute for the Future, although an exact percentage is impossible to predict. The IFTF, an organization that seeks to identify emerging trends and their impacts on global society, forecasts that many of the tasks and duties of the jobs that today's young people will hold in 2030 don't exist right now.

"Those who plan to work for the next 50 years have to have a mindset of, 'I'm going to be working and learning and working and learning, and working and learning,' in order to make a career," says Rachel Maguire, a research director with IFTF. By 2030, we'll likely be living in a world where artificial assistants help us with almost every task, not unlike the way email tries to finish spelling a word for users today. Maguire says it will be like having an assistant working alongside you, taking on tasks at which the human brain does not excel.

The U.S. Bureau of Labor Statistics says today's students will have eight to 10 jobs by the time they are 38. And they won't necessarily have to take time away from any one of those jobs for training or to gain additional qualifications related to their fields. Instead, they'll partner with machines for on-the-job learning, wearing an augmented reality headset that will give them the information they need in real-time to get the work done. "It eliminates the need for people to leave a job in order to learn a new skill so they can level up and earn more money," Maguire says. "It gives the opportunity for people to be able to learn those kinds of new skills and demonstrate proficiency in-the-moment at the job."

And forget about traditional human resources departments or the challenging task of looking for a job on your own. In the future, the job might come to you. Potential employers will draw from different data sources, including online business profiles and social media streams, to find out about a person and their skills. Maguire says there's already a lot of activity around turning employment into a matchmaking endeavor, using artificial intelligence and deep learning to help the right person and the right job find each other.

In theory, this kind of online job matching could lead to less bias and discrimination in hiring practices. However, there are potential pitfalls. "We have to make sure that the people who are building these tools aren't informing these tools with their own biases, whether they're intentional or not," Maguire says. "These systems will only be as good as the data that feeds them."

Which leads Maguire to another point. While she doesn't want to sound melodramatic about emerging technologies, she believes it is critical for the public to get engaged now, rather than sitting back and letting technology happen to them. "What do we want from these new technological capabilities, and how do we make sure we put in place the social policies and systems that will result in what it is we all want?" she says. "I have a deep concern that we're just kind of sitting back and letting technology tell us what jobs we'll have and what jobs we won't have, rather than us figuring out how to apply these technologies to improve our lives."

▸音読10回CHECK 1 ☐ 2 ☐ 3 ☐ 4 ☐ 5 ☐ 6 ☐ 7 ☐ 8 ☐ 9 ☐ 10 ☐

BACKGROUND KNOWLEDGE

AIで生まれる仕事

本書と同じシリーズである**『大学入試　レベル別英語長文問題　ソリューション最新テーマ編1 スタンダードレベル』**の第5問で、**「AIに奪われる仕事と残る仕事」**というタイトルでAIに関するコラムを紹介しました。本コラムでは、**新たにAIで生まれる仕事を紹介したい**と思います。この第5問にあったように、**過去の産業革命でも、IT革命でも、新たに多くの仕事が生まれました。**AI革命が起きると仮定して、なくなる仕事よりも、生まれる仕事に目を向けていきたいと思います。

まずは、**Data Detective「データ探偵」**と言われる仕事です。**データ調査の専門家**として、**PCやスマートフォンなどのIoT機器から収集したデータを調査**します。これは、**AIが得意な統計や分析の能力を生かして、そのデータをどのように活用するか、アイデアを出す仕事**です。

次に、**AI Business Development Manager「AI 事業開発責任者」**と言われる仕事です。**AIを活用して、どのように事業として成立させていくか、収入、支出、事業計画を立てる責任者が必要**になります。通常の事業開発の仕事に、AIの専門知識を備えることが必要な仕事です。

最後は、意外に思われるかもしれませんが、**「散歩・会話の相手」**です。**AIの普及により人との触れ合いが減少する中**で、本書の問題10で扱う**孤独問題**や**高齢化社会**の影響もあいまって、話し相手がとても貴重になる時代がくると予測できます。**散歩を時間単位で一緒にしてくれる人、会話も時間単位で一緒にしてくれる人、そのサービスに対価を払う時代がやってくる可能性があります。**

問題 6

IT・テクノロジー

自動運転車

別冊p.22／制限時間25分／561 words

解答

(1) 2　(2) 4　(3) 3　(4) 4　(5) 3
(6) 1　(7) 1　(8) 2　(9) 4　(10) 1

解説

(1)

1 ～として　2 ～のように　3 ～と違って　4 ～なしで

空欄(　a　)が含まれる文は、(　a　) many over-optimistic images of the future, it is a bit of an illusionとなる。**many over-optimistic images「多くの楽観的過ぎるイメージ」**と、**a bit of an illusion「やや幻想だ」**はどちらもマイナスイメージで**同義**なので、**2 like**が正解となる。

(2)

4は**第2段落最終文That is what appears to have happened in the crash.「それがその衝突で起きたように思えることだ」**から、**断定を避けている表現と一致する**ので正解。

不正解の選択肢を見ていくと、1は**第2段落第4文の途中 many automated cars on the road today still require someone to be there in case of an emergency「今日(こんにち)の道路を走る多くの自動運転車は、まだ緊急時に誰かがそこにいることを必要とする」に反する**ので不適。2は同文で、**the person in the driver's seat ―～ ― may also fail to intervene「運転席の人が介入できないかもしれない」**とあるだけで**2の「責任がある」との表現はない**ので、不適。3は「誤作動」との表記は本文中にない。

(3)

1 自動運転車の背後で、そのテクノロジーによって誘発される危険に関する懸念を表明する人はほとんどいない。

2 これらの近代的、かつ強力な乗り物で使用される新しいテクノロジーを理解している人はほとんどいない。

3 これらの新しい車で使われるテクノロジーは、予測が難しい事故を引き起こすかもしれない。

4 これらの近代的な車で使われるテクノロジーは、とても強力なので、正しく評価されない。

構文図解

the technology (that powers these vehicles) could introduce new risks (that few people appreciate).

the technology = S / (that powers these vehicles) = M（関係代名詞のthat）/ could introduce = V / new risks = O / (that few people appreciate) = M（関係代名詞のthat）

1つ目のthatから**関係代名詞**のカタマリが始まり、vehiclesまでの**形容詞節**を作り、the technologyを修飾する。that節内の**powersは動詞**で、「**～を（動力で）動かす**」の意味。the technologyがS、could introduceがV、new risksがOの第3文型の文。2つ目のthatも**関係代名詞**でappreciateまでの**形容詞節**を作り、new risksを修飾する。**few**は「**ほとんど～ない**」と**数を打ち消す準否定語**であることに注意する。

まとめると「**これらの乗り物を動かすテクノロジーは、ほとんどの人が正しく認識できない新しいリスクを生み出すことになるだろう**」となるので、**3 The technology used in these new cars may cause accidents that are difficult to predict.**が正解。本文の**few people appreciate**が、3の**difficult to predict**にパラフレーズされていることに注意する。

(4)

1 (d) 持ち込む (e) 持ち込む
2 (d) 持ち込む (e) 変える
3 (d) 変える (e) 変える
4 (d) 変える (e) 持ち込む

空所(d)と(e)が含まれている文は、Technology does not eliminate error, but it (　d　) the nature of errors that are made, and it (　e　) new kinds of errors「テクノロジーはエラーをなくすのではなく、起きるエラーの性質を(　d　)、新しい種類のエラーを(　e　)」となる。下線部(c) the technology ~ could **introduce new risks** ~ . から、(e)にはintroducesが入るとわかるので、1、4が正解の候補になる。空所(d)は**目的語がthe nature of errors「エラーの性質」**なので、introduce「持ち込む」ではなくてchange「変える」がふさわしいとわかる。not A but Bの対比構造にも注意する。

(5)

1　確立された理論　　　2　隠された思い込み
3　証明されていない仮説　　4　間違った状況

空所(f)が含まれている文は、~ under the (　f　) that the technology will reduce crashes and fatalities.となる。thatは**同格のthat**で、**同格とは前後イコール関係**なので、(　f　) = the technology will reduce crashes and fatalities「**テクノロジーが衝突や事故死を減らすだろう**」となる。**第2段落の下線部(c)**、**第3段落第1文**から、「**テクノロジーが衝突や事故死を減らすだろう**」は、**3 unproven hypothesis「証明されていない仮説」が正解**とわかる。

(6)

1　確信のある　　2　疑念を抱いている
3　実際に認識する　　4　理解しない

下線部(g)を含む文は、**Even as officials (g) place a big bet that autonomous cars will solve many of our safety problems,** ~ .「**役人たちが、自動運転車が私たちの安全上の問題の多くを解決するだろうと、大きな賭けに出ているときでさえも**」となる。「**大きな賭けに出る**」とは「**確信のある**」ことなので、**1. are confident**が正解。

(7)

1　連邦及び州議会議員は、未来の命を救うための法案を準備するのに時間を費やしてきたけれども
2　将来のリスクに関して、もっと深刻な懸念があるだろうと専門家が警告したから

3　公務員が将来の死亡率の増加に反対すべきとき
4　しかし、それにもかかわらず、彼らは死亡事故のない明るい未来を期待する

下線部(h)を含む文は、**In the federal government and most states, there appears to be little interest in making policies with proven track records of saving lives now,** (h) **as opposed to some time in the distant future.**「**連邦政府やほとんどの州で、遠い将来のある時にではなく、今、命を救う証明済みの実績ある政策を立案することに、ほとんど興味がないように見える**」となる。

as opposed toは「**～とは対照的に**」と**対比**を表すので、下線部(h)は「**連邦政府やほとんどの州で、遠い将来のある時に命を救う証明済みの実績ある政策を立案する**」ことを意味する。よって、**1. although federal and state lawmakers have spent time preparing bills to save lives in the future**が正解とわかる。**make policy**「**政策を立案する**」が**prepare bill**「**法案を準備する**」と同義であることに注意する。

論理 POINT ❸ 対比の目印

本問で登場したような**対比を発見する目印と**なる表現をまとめます。
as opposed to「**～に対して**」／ **rather than**「**～よりむしろ**」
instead of「**～する代わりに**」／ **in contrast to**「**～とは対照的に**」

(8)

1　これらの国の中には、車の流れの速度を落とそうと努めてきた国もある。
2　これらの国は歩行者が車にあまり注意を払わなくてもいいように、道路に変化をもたらした。
3　ヨーロッパの規制者は、後部座席にも目に見える注意書きを貼って、シートベルトの使用を促している。
4　ドイツは、ほとんどのアメリカの州が行うよりもずっと厳格な運転教習や試験を要求している。

交通事故を減らすのに、**1 スピードの制限**、**3 シートベルトの着用**、

4 厳しい運転教習や試験は理にかなっているが、**2**の「**歩行者が車に注意を払わない**」のは、**交通事故を減らす手段として合理的とは言えない**ので、2が正解となる。

(9)

1 政府はこうした問題を修正できるほど素早く動いていないし、産業界も動いていない
2 自動車産業は、将来ではなく、今お金を稼ぐ必要がある
3 自動運転車は、それが原因で、禁止も規制もされるべきではない
4 私たちは最速の方法ではなくて、責任ある方法でそれを行う必要がある

空所(j)を含む文は、**"Even though there is a sense of urgency to prevent human-caused accidents, (j)."**「**人間が引き起こす事故を防ぐのに、緊急性はあるけれども、(j)**」となる。すると、**urgency**と**though**の**譲歩構造でつなぐ**には、「**緊急性はあるけれども、しっかりした方法で**」という文脈がふさわしいとわかる。よって、**in a responsible way, not the fastest way**「**最速の方法ではなくて、責任のある方法で**」を含む4が正解とわかる。**not A but B**が変形した**B, not A**「**AではなくてB**」に注意する。

(10)

1 自動運転車の時代？ まず考えてみよう
2 アメリカの道路を再び安全にすること
3 自動運転車の可能性と将来性
4 交通制御の方法の新旧対決

この文章のテーマである「**自動運転車**」が入っている1と3に正解の候補を絞る。この文章では、繰り返し**自動運転車の**「**危険性**」について述べているので、**3のpotential**「**可能性**」や**promise**「**将来性**」**というプラスイメージだけのタイトルは不適**。**1のように疑問形を使用して、しっかり考えることを促すタイトルがふさわしい**ので、1が正解となる。

構 文 図 解

The promise (of self-driving cars) can be attractive. Imagine
S　M　V　C　V

〈taking a nap〉 or 〈watching a movie〉 [in a comfortable armchair
動名詞　O　動名詞　O　M　前置詞のlike

while being shuttled safely home after a long day at work]. But [like
you（一般人を表す）are の省略　仕事後に安全に送ってもらいながら快適な椅子で仮眠を取ることや映画を観ること

many over-optimistic images of the future], it is (a bit of) an illusion.
M　S　V　M　C

Automated cars may indeed make commuting more pleasurable
S　V　O　C

[while preventing accidents and saving many lives — someday]. But
M　they（automated cars）areの省略

a recent fatal crash suggests 〈that some of these cars are not ready
S　V　名詞節のthat　O　automated carsを指す

for the busy American roads〉: a lot of sensors and software turned
S　V

this car [into a high-tech vehicle you might see in a science fiction
O　turn A into B　関係詞の省略　M

movie]. [In fact], the technology (that powers these vehicles) could
M　S　関係代名詞のthat　M　V

introduce new risks (that few people appreciate). [For example],
O　関係代名詞のthat　M　M

[when a computer controlling the car does not hit the brakes to avoid
M　現在分詞の後置修飾　不定詞 副詞的用法

a car crash], the person (in the driver's seat) — many automated
S　M　M

cars on the road today still require someone to be there in case of an
the person がS　require O to doのto do

emergency — may also fail to intervene [because the driver trusts
V　コンピューターが作動しないときに運転席の人が不注意で介入できないこと

the car too much to pay close attention to the road]. That is 〈what
M　too ~ to ...　S　V　関係代名詞のwhat

appears to have happened in the crash〉.
C

本文訳

自動運転車の将来性は魅力的に思えることがある。長時間仕事をした後に、家まで安全に運んでくれる間に、快適な肘掛け椅子で仮眠を取ることや、映画を観ることを想像してみよう。しかし、未来への楽観的過ぎる多くのイメージと同様に、それはやや幻想である。
自動運転車は、いつの日か事故を防ぎ多くの命を救いながら、実際に通勤をより快適なものにするかもしれない。しかし、最近の致命的な事故は、こうした車のいくつかは交通量の多いアメリカの道路に対応できていないことを示す。たくさんのセンサーやソフトウェアが、この車をSF映画で見るようなハイテクな乗り物へと変えた。実際に、これらの乗り物を動かすテクノロジーは、ほとんどの人が正しく認識できない新しいリスクを生み出すことになるだろう。例えば、車を制御するコンピューターが、車との衝突を避けるのにブレーキを踏まないとき、今日の道路を走る多くの自動運転車は、まだ緊急時に誰かが運転席にいることを必要とするが、運転席の人もまた車を信頼し過ぎて道路にしっかりと注意を払うことができず、（事故防止に）介入できないかもしれない。それが衝突の際に起きたように思えることだ。

語彙リスト

□ promise	名	将来性
□ self-driving	形	自動運転の
□ attractive	形	魅力的な
□ take a nap	熟	仮眠を取る
□ comfortable	形	快適な
□ armchair	名	肘掛け椅子
□ shuttle	動	往復運転で運ぶ
□ optimistic	形	楽観的な
□ a bit of	熟	やや～
□ illusion	名	幻想
□ automated	形	自動化された
□ indeed	副	実際に
□ commute	動	通勤する
□ pleasurable	形	快適な
□ prevent	動	防ぐ
□ save	動	救う
□ fatal	形	致命的な
□ crash	名	衝突
□ be ready for	熟	～の準備ができている
□ turn A into B	熟	AをBに変える
□ vehicle	名	乗り物
□ power	動	～を動力で動かす
□ introduce	動	持ち込む
□ risk	名	リスク
□ appreciate	動	認識する
□ hit the brake	熟	ブレーキを踏む
□ avoid	動	避ける
□ require O to do	熟	Oに～するように要求する
□ in case of an emergency	熟	緊急時に
□ intervene	動	介入する
□ pay attention to	熟	～に注意を払う
□ appear to do	熟	～するように思える

▸単語10回CHECK 1 □ 2 □ 3 □ 4 □ 5 □ 6 □ 7 □ 8 □ 9 □ 10 □

構文図解

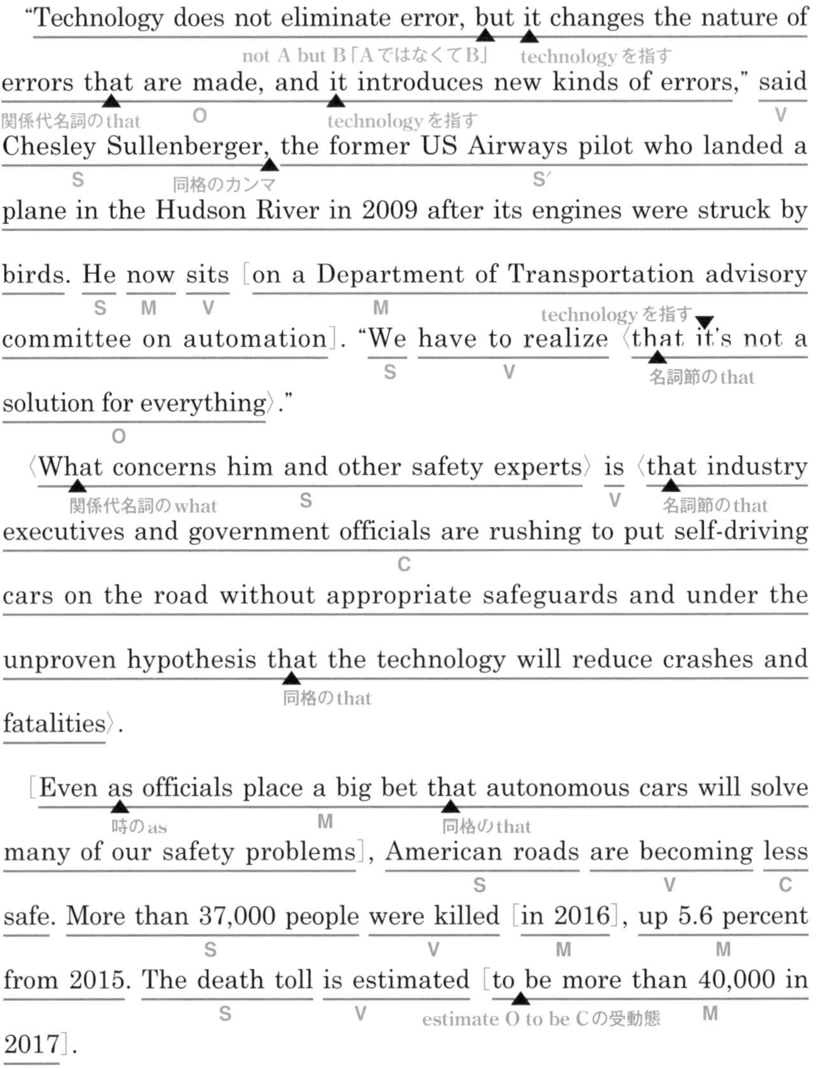
"Technology does not eliminate error, but it changes the nature of errors that are made, and it introduces new kinds of errors," said Chesley Sullenberger, the former US Airways pilot who landed a plane in the Hudson River in 2009 after its engines were struck by birds. He now sits [on a Department of Transportation advisory committee on automation]. "We have to realize 〈that it's not a solution for everything〉."
not A but B「AではなくてB」
technologyを指す
関係代名詞のthat
O
technologyを指す
V
S
同格のカンマ
S′
S
M
V
M
technologyを指す
S
V
名詞節のthat
O
〈What concerns him and other safety experts〉 is 〈that industry executives and government officials are rushing to put self-driving cars on the road without appropriate safeguards and under the unproven hypothesis that the technology will reduce crashes and fatalities〉.
関係代名詞のwhat
S
V
名詞節のthat
C
同格のthat
[Even as officials place a big bet that autonomous cars will solve many of our safety problems], American roads are becoming less safe. More than 37,000 people were killed [in 2016], up 5.6 percent from 2015. The death toll is estimated [to be more than 40,000 in 2017].
時のas
M
同格のthat
S
V
C
S
V
M
M
S
V
estimate O to be Cの受動態
M

本文訳

「テクノロジーはエラーをなくすのではなく、起きるエラーの性質を変えたり、新しい種類のエラーを持ち込んだりする」と、2009年にエンジンに鳥がぶつかった後に、ハドソン川に飛行機を不時着させた前USエアウェイズのパイロットであるチェズレイ・サレンバーガーが言った。彼は今、運輸省の自動運転化の*諮問（しもん）委員会の一員だ。「私たちは、それがすべてに対する解決策ではないと認識しなければならない」。

彼や他の安全の専門家を不安にさせるものは、業界幹部や政府役人が、適切な安全装置なしに、かつテクノロジーで衝突や事故死を減らせるだろうという証明されていない仮説のもと、自動運転車を路上で走らせることを急いでいることだ。

自動運転車が私たちの安全上の問題の多くを解決するだろうと、役人たちが大きな賭けに出ているときでさえも、アメリカの道路は、ますます安全ではなくなりつつある。3万7千人以上の人が、2016年に亡くなって、それは2015年より5.6%増加した。死傷者数は、2017年には4万人を超えると推測される。

*「諮問委員会」は、政治上の重要問題決定の際などに参考とする、専門的見解を有する学者や専門家の集まりのこと。

語彙リスト

eliminate	動	削除する
error	名	間違い
former	形	前の
land	動	着陸させる
strike	動	ぶつかる
advisory committee	名	諮問委員会
automation	名	自動化
solution	名	解決策
concern	動	心配させる
expert	名	専門家
executive	名	(経営)幹部
government official	名	政府役人
safeguard	名	安全装置
hypothesis	名	仮説
fatality	名	(事故などによる)死亡者(数)
place a big bet	熟	大きな賭けをする
autonomous	形	自動の
toll	名	死傷者数
estimate	動	推測する

▸単語10回CHECK 1 2 3 4 5 6 7 8 9 10

構文図解

Experts (who are skeptical about the unstoppable march of technology) say 〈fatalities are rising because public officials have become so fond of the shiny new thing that they have taken their eyes off problems they could be solving today〉. [In the federal government and most states], there appears to be little interest (in making policies with proven track records of saving lives now), [as opposed to some time in the distant future].

S: Experts / M: (who are skeptical about the unstoppable march of technology) / V: say / O: 〈fatalities ... today〉
say ▲ 名詞節のthatの省略
that ▲ so ～ that ... のthat
they ▲ public officials を指す
problems ▼ 関係詞の省略
they ▲ public officials を指す
M: [In the federal government and most states] / M: there / V: appears to be / S: little interest / M: (in making ... now)
making ▲ 動名詞
saving ▲ 動名詞
M: [as opposed to some time in the distant future]
future ▲ now との時の対比

Other industrialized countries have made great progress (in reducing traffic crashes over the last two decades). Road fatality rates (in Canada, France, Germany and Sweden), [for example], are now less [than half the rate in the United States]. And no, these countries don't have (loads of) self-driving cars. They have reduced accidents [in the old-fashioned way]. Some (of them) have worked [to slow down traffic]; speed is a leading killer. They have made changes [to roads] [so pedestrians will not have to pay much attention to cars]. European regulators have encouraged the use (of seatbelts) [by putting visual reminders even in the back seat]. Germany requires much more rigorous driver education and testing [than most American states do].

S: Other industrialized countries / V: have made / O: great progress / M: (in reducing ... decades)
reducing ▲ 動名詞
S: Road fatality rates / M: (in Canada, France, Germany and Sweden) / M: [for example] / V: are / M: now / C: less / M: [than half the rate in the United States]
and ▲ Canada ～ Sweden の4つの接続
these ▲ Canada ～ Sweden を指す
S: these countries / V: don't have / M: (loads of) / O: self-driving cars
They ▼ these countries を指す
S: They / V: have reduced / O: accidents / M: [in the old-fashioned way]
them ▼ these countries を指す
S: Some / M: (of them) / V: have worked / M: [to slow down traffic]
to slow ▲ 不定詞 副詞的用法
S: speed / V: is / C: a leading killer
They ▼ these countries を指す
S: They / V: have made / O: changes / M: [to roads] / M: [so pedestrians ... cars]
so ▲ so that S 助動詞 のthatの省略
S: European regulators / V: have encouraged / O: the use / M: (of seatbelts) / M: [by putting ... back seat]
putting ▲ 動名詞
S: Germany / V: requires / O: much more rigorous driver education and testing / M: [than most American states do]
much ▲ 比較級の強調
do ▲ requires ～ testing の代動詞

本文訳

テクノロジーの止められない行進に懐疑的な専門家は、死傷者数が増えているのは、公務員が新しく、輝くようなものがとても好きになってしまって、自分たちが今日解決できる問題から目をそらしているせいだと言う。連邦政府やほとんどの州で、遠い将来のある時にではなく、今、命を救う証明済みの実績ある政策を立案することに、ほとんど興味がないように見える。

他の先進国は、過去20年で、交通事故を減らすのに大きな進歩を遂げてきた。例えば、カナダ、フランス、ドイツ、スウェーデンの道路での死傷者率は、今ではアメリカの半分以下だ。そして、なんとこれらの国には、多くの自動運転車があるわけではない。これらの国は、昔ながらのやり方で、事故を減らしてきた。なかには、車の流れの速度を落とそうと努めてきた国もある。スピードが最も大きな死因の1つだ。それらの諸国は、歩行者が車に多くの注意を払わなくてもいいように、道路に変化をほどこした。ヨーロッパの規制者は、後部座席にも目に見える注意書きを貼って、シートベルトの利用を促した。ドイツは、ほとんどのアメリカの州が行うよりもずっと、厳格な運転教習と試験を要求している。

語彙リスト

□	skeptical	形 懐疑的な
□	march	名 行進
□	public official	名 公務員
□	be fond of	熟 ～が好きだ
□	shiny	形 輝く
□	federal government	名 連邦政府
□	track record	名 実績
□	as opposed to	熟 ～と対照的に
□	make progress	熟 進歩する
□	traffic	形 交通の
□	loads of	熟 たくさんの～
□	old-fashioned	形 昔風の
□	work	動 努力する
□	leading	形 主要な
□	pedestrian	名 歩行者
□	regulator	名 規制者
□	visual	形 目に見える
□	reminder	名 注意書き
□	rigorous	形 厳格な

▸単語10回CHECK 1 □ 2 □ 3 □ 4 □ 5 □ 6 □ 7 □ 8 □ 9 □ 10 □

構文図解

Mr. Sullenberger is worried 〈that the rush to develop automated cars will lead to many unforeseen problems〉. "［Even though there is a sense of urgency to prevent human-caused accidents］, we need to do it ［in a responsible way, not the fastest way］."

S: Mr. Sullenberger / V: is worried / O: 〈that ... problems〉（名詞節のthat）/ to develop: 不定詞 形容詞的用法

M: ［Even though ... accidents］/ to prevent: 不定詞 形容詞的用法 / S: we / V: need to do / O: it（prevent human-caused accidentsを指す）/ M: ［in a responsible way, not the fastest way］（B, not A）

本文訳

サレンバーガー氏は、自動運転車を急いで開発することは、多くの予見できない問題につながるだろうと心配している。「人間が引き起こす事故を防ぐのに、緊急性はあるけれども、私たちは、最速の方法ではなくて、責任のある方法でそれを行う必要がある」。

語彙リスト

rush	名 急ぐこと	unforeseen	形 予見できない
lead to	熟 ～につながる	responsible	形 責任のある

▸単語10回CHECK 1 2 3 4 5 6 7 8 9 10

The promise of self-driving cars can be attractive. Imagine taking a nap or watching a movie in a comfortable armchair while being shuttled safely home after a long day at work. But like many over-optimistic images of the future, it is a bit of an illusion.

Automated cars may indeed make commuting more pleasurable while preventing accidents and saving many lives — someday. But a recent fatal crash suggests that some of these cars are not ready for the busy American roads: a lot of sensors and software turned this car into a high-tech vehicle you might see in a science fiction movie. In fact, the technology that powers these vehicles could introduce new risks that few people appreciate. For example, when a computer controlling the car does not hit the brakes to avoid a car crash, the person in the driver's seat — many automated cars on the road today still require someone to be there in case of an emergency — may also fail to intervene because the driver trusts the car too much to pay close attention to the road. That is what appears to have happened in the crash.

"Technology does not eliminate error, but it changes the nature of errors that are made, and it introduces new kinds of errors," said Chesley Sullenberger, the former US Airways pilot who landed a plane in the Hudson River in 2009 after its engines were struck by birds. He now sits on a Department of Transportation advisory committee on automation. "We have to realize that it's not a solution for everything."

What concerns him and other safety experts is that industry executives and government officials are rushing to put self-driving cars on the road without appropriate safeguards and under the unproven hypothesis that the technology will reduce crashes and fatalities.

Even as officials place a big bet that autonomous cars will solve many of our safety problems, American roads are becoming less safe. More than 37,000 people were killed in 2016, up 5.6 percent from 2015. The death toll is estimated to be more than 40,000 in 2017.

Experts who are skeptical about the unstoppable march of technology say fatalities are rising because public officials have become so fond of the shiny new thing that they have taken their eyes off problems they could be solving today. In the federal government and most states, there appears to be little interest in making policies with proven track records of saving lives now, as opposed to some time in the distant future.

Other industrialized countries have made great progress in reducing traffic crashes over the last two decades. Road fatality rates in Canada, France, Germany and Sweden, for example, are now less than half the rate in the United States. And no, these countries don't have loads of self-driving cars. They have reduced accidents in the old-fashioned way. Some of them have worked to slow down traffic; speed is a leading killer. European regulators have encouraged the use of seatbelts by putting visual reminders even in the back seat. Germany requires much more rigorous driver education and testing than most American states do.

Mr. Sullenberger is worried that the rush to develop automated cars will lead to many unforeseen problems. "Even though there is a sense of urgency to prevent human-caused accidents, we need to do it in a responsible way, not the fastest way."

▶音読10回CHECK 1 2 3 4 5 6 7 8 9 10

背景知識が
広がるコラム

BACKGROUND KNOWLEDGE

自動運転車の功罪

近年、世界中で開発が進んでいる自動運転車を、功罪というプラスとマイナスの観点で見ていきましょう。

自動運転車のメリットとして、第一に**人が運転から解放される**ことが挙げられるでしょう。自動運転が実現すれば人は運転しないので、**乗車中に読書をしたり仕事をしたりと時間を有効活用することができます**。お酒を飲んでいても、自動運転車なら車が家まで送り届けてくれるので、**飲酒運転もなくす**ことができます。

第二に、意外に思われるかもしれませんが、**交通事故の減少**です。完全な実用化はまだ先なので、自動運転車の試験段階での事故が発生しています。しかし、実用化された自動運転車は、常にコンピューターによって制御され、運転されるので、**ドライバーの操作ミスや確認不足、判断ミスといった、従来の人為的な要因による交通事故を減らす**ことができます。

一方、**自動運転車のデメリット**も複数存在します。1つ目は、**事故発生時の責任を誰が負えばいいのかわからない**という点です。**車の搭乗者が負うのか、システムの開発者が負うのか**、事故後の争点となる可能性が出てきます。

さらに、**外部からのハッキングによる悪用の可能性**です。自動運転のシステムがハッキングされると、**テロや犯罪行為、戦争などに使われる可能性**があります。
あらゆる問題で、“功”と“罪”という視点を大切にしてください。

問題

7

環　境

傘のゴミを減らす

別冊 p.28 ／制限時間 25 分／ 558 words

解答

問1 a　問2 c　問3 c　問4 b

問5 1 d　2 f　3 g　4 e　5 c　6 a

問6 e　問7 d　問8 e　問9 c, f

解説

問1

a. 捨てられた　b. 中止された　c. 終わった　d. 排出された
e. 取りかえられた

discard「**捨てる**」は**dis**「**離れて**」＋ **card**「**カード**」が語源で、「**トランプのカードを離れたところにやる**」＝「**捨てる**」となったもの。「**捨てる**」のパラフレーズは頻出で、**throw away, get rid of, remove, discard, abandon** などがよくパラフレーズされる。よって **a. abandoned** が正解。

問2

a. 利用者は、傘をお土産として取っておきたい観光客だ。
b. 利用者は、スマートフォンの画面上で、QR コードリーダーを必要としている。
c. 利用者は、インターネットを経由して、街中で傘を借りることができる。
d. 利用者は、最も近い場所で傘の種類をチェックできる。
e. 利用者は、クレジットカードを登録してから、そのサービスを無料で利用できる。

c は、**第 3 段落第 1 文 Users of the service register with the company via the LINE messaging app and check for the umbrella spots closest to their location.**「**そのサービスの利用者**

は、LINEのメッセージアプリを経由してその会社に登録して、自分たちの場所に最も近い傘置き場を調べる」のvia the LINE messaging appがcのthrough the Internetにパラフレーズされて**同義**なので、正解。

不正解の選択肢を見ていくと、aは本文に記述なし。bは、**第3段落第2文The user goes to the stand,** unlocks their umbrella of choice **by scanning the QR code on its handle** ～.「**利用者はその傘置き場に行き、選んだ傘の取っ手のQRコードを読み取り、**～」から、スマートフォンのQRコードリーダーが必要であろうが、それがアイカサそのものの説明ではないので、不適。

dは、第3段落第1文より「傘の**場所**を確認する」とあるだけで、「傘の**種類**を確認する」とは書いていないので不適。eは、**同段落最終文for 70 yen per day「1日につき70円」**とあり、eの**for free「無料で」と反する**ので不適。

問3

a. アイカサの会社は、インターネットでその傘の場所を確認し続けている。
b. アイカサのシステムは、15の都道府県に位置する場所に、利用者が傘を戻すことを要求する。
c. そのサービスは、登録したクレジットカード情報で利用者を特定する。
d. そのサービスは、利用者が現金で払い忘れた場合に備えて、クレジットカードの登録を要求する。
e. その利用者は、事前に傘を何日借りるのかを登録して、1日につき70円支払う。

下線部(ウ)の後ろにある**理由のsince**に着目する。**since the registration of credit card numbers connects the umbrellas to the personal information of users「(アイカサのシステムは) クレジットカード番号の登録が、傘と利用者の個人情報を結び付けることになって」**から、c. **The service identifies the users through the credit card information that they registered.**が正解。

不正解の選択肢を見ていくと、a, bは本文に記述なし。

1 健康 2 心理 3 IT・テクノロジー 4 健康 5 IT・テクノロジー 6 IT・テクノロジー 7 環境 8 文化 9 環境 10 社会

dは第3段落最終文とThe service ～ credit cardまでが合致するが、**just in case they forget to pay in cash「利用者が現金で払い忘れる場合に備えて」**とは書かれていないので不適。eは本文に記述なし。

問4

a. 日本洋傘振興協議会は、日本で共有する傘の数を間違って計算した。

b. 函館商工会議所は、傘の共有システムを提供することで、観光客を助けようとした。

c. 北海道新幹線の駅は、もっと利益を上げるために、2,300本の傘を売りに出した。

d. 東京の渋谷区は、観光客に2016年から傘を貸し出したが、利用できる傘を使い切ってしまった。

e. 大阪の飲料メーカーは、自動販売機の隣に無料で使用できる傘を配置したが、利用者はめったに同じ場所には戻さなかった。

bは、**第5段落第2文the Hakodate Chamber of Commerce and Industry ～ made 2,300 umbrellas available for free use by tourists「北海道の函館商工会議所が、～2,300本の傘を、観光客が無料で使用できるようにした」**と一致するので正解。

不正解の選択肢を見ていくと、aは本文に記述なし。cは**第5段落第2文**に反するので不適。dは**第5段落最終文**で「同じ理由（傘の低い返却率）で失敗した」とあるだけで、利用できる傘を使い切ったとは書かれていないので不適。eは本文に記述なし。

問5

下線部(オ)を含む文は**The tourism promotion program ended a year later because (オ)(_____).** なので、**「その事業が1年で終わった理由」**が下線部(オ)に入るとわかる。選択肢から**「傘がほとんど返却されなかった」**と推測できるので、**few of the umbrellas had been returned（d-f-g-e-c-a）**が正解の文となる。bのmostが使用されない単語。

問6

a. 役立つサービスへと変わったビジネス
b. 鉄道のスケジュールを支援する構造
c. 組織を支援するものとみなされる人のグループ
d. 建物の土台となる天然の、あるいは準備された土地
e. 社会が機能するのに必要な基本システムやサービス

下線部(カ)の後ろにあるsuch asに着目する。**such asの後ろは具体例が続く**ので、**infrastructure**の具体例は、**Japan's excellent railway network「日本のすぐれた鉄道網」**とわかる。infrastructureは日本語では「**インフラ**」と呼ばれ、**水道・電気・鉄道・学校などの社会基盤**を意味するので、**e. the basic systems and services needed for a society to functionが正解**になる。bは鉄道のスケジュールを支援することに限定されているわけではないので不適。

論理 POINT ④ 具体例の目印

本問で登場したような**具体例を発見する目印**となる表現をまとめます。
for example (instance)「例えば」/ **such as**「～のような」/ **including**「～を含めて」/ **固有名詞・具体的な数字** / **3つ以上の情報の接続**

問7

a. ～のなすがままに　b. ～と対照的に　c. ～に反対して
d. ～に合わせて　e. ～の寸前で

空欄キを含む文は、**The Tokyo-based venture company said it developed the new material [キ] global trends toward reducing plastic use for environmental protection.**「**東京拠点のそのベンチャー企業は、環境保護のためにプラスチックの使用を減らす世界的な傾向 [キ]、その新しい素材を開発したと述べた**」となる。すると、「プラスチックを減らす世界的な傾向**に合わせて**新しい素材を開発した」と推測できるので、**d. in line with「～に合わせて」**が正解となる。

問8

a. 傘を返す時に、自動販売機から飲み物を買うこと
b. 傘を無料で使用できる自分の家に最も近い場所を選ぶこと
c. 払い戻しを受けるために、できる限り早く借りた傘を返すこと
d. 電車や駅に置き忘れた傘を集めて捨てること
e. レンタル傘サービスを使って常に傘を返すこと

eは、本文の**アイカサのサービスそのもの**で、**これにより傘のゴミを減らすことができる**ので正解。

不正解の選択肢を見ていくと、a, bはゴミを減らす方法にはならないので不適。cは「払い戻しを受けるために」という目的部分が不適。dは**第7段落第2文、第3文**で、電車に置き忘れた傘は大阪の飲料メーカーが利用しており、むしろ再利用すべき対象なので不適。

問9

a. 日本人の大多数は、突然雨が降った時、共有傘を借りる。
b. 日本では毎年およそ8,000万本のビニール傘が購入されている。
c. ある新興企業が、傘のゴミを減らすのにIoTのテクノロジーを利用している。
d. 北海道の鉄道会社が、東京のアイカサのサービスと業務提携を結んだ。
e. アイカサのサービスが使用する傘には、鉄道会社が提供する、バスやオフィスに置き忘れたものがある。
f. 環境を保護するために、ベンチャー企業は新しく開発された素材で作った傘をすぐに使うだろう。
g. ライメックスは、新しい顧客に傘を提供するクレジットカード会社だ。

解法 POINT ❹ 内容一致問題の解法（5つ以上の選択肢）

5つ以上の選択肢がある内容一致問題は、**段落を2つ読むごとに選択肢を処理する**ことをおすすめします。

cは**第2段落第1文A start-up company ～, using “Internet of Things”(IoT) technology to reduce umbrella waste.**と一致する

ので正解。fは**第8段落第1文後半using umbrellas made of Limex, an innovative material、同段落第2文後半for environmental protectionより正解。**

不正解の選択肢を見ていくと、aは、**第1段落第2文Many people buy new umbrellas when it suddenly rains.「突然雨が降ると、新しい傘を買う人がたくさんいる」**に反するので不適。

bは、**同段落第4文While 120 to 130 million umbrellas are sold per year in Japan, approximately 80 million plastic ones are discarded annually「日本では年間1億2千万～1億3千万本の傘が販売されているが、～、毎年およそ8,000万本のビニール傘が捨てられている」から、bの8000万という数字は捨てられているビニール傘の数なので不適。**

dは本文に記述なし。eは**第7段落第3文**で「電車や駅に置き忘れた傘を無料貸し出しするサービス」が出てくるが、アイカサのサービスではないので不適。gは**第8段落第1文後半**より、Limexとは素材を指すので不適。

1 健康
2 心理
3 IT・テクノロジー
4 健康
5 IT・テクノロジー
6 IT・テクノロジー
7 環境
8 文化
9 環境
10 社会

構文図解

不定詞 名詞的用法

[Generally speaking], Japanese people do not really like ⟨to get

M S V O

wet⟩ [when it rains]. Many people buy new umbrellas [when it

M S V O M

関係代名詞のas

suddenly rains]. [As is often the case with the newly bought ones],

the newly bought onesを指す M umbrellasを指す

they end up [being left] [in various places]. [While 120 to 130

S V M M M

million umbrellas are sold per year in Japan], approximately 80

S

million plastic ones are discarded annually, [according to the Japan

umbrellasを指す V M M

Umbrella Promotion Association and other sources].

A start-up company has successfully launched an umbrella-sharing

S V O

service, [mainly in Tokyo], [using "Internet of Things" (IoT)

M 分詞構文 M

technology to reduce umbrella waste]. The company started the

不定詞 副詞的用法 The companyを指す S V O

service [in December 2018], and it aims for the use (of all rented

M S V O M

umbrellas). The service is called iKasa [since "Kasa" is Japanese for

S V C M 「～を表す」

umbrella].

Users (of the service) register [with the company] [via the LINE

S M V M M

messaging app] and check for the umbrella spots (closest to their

V O 形容詞の後置修飾

location). The user goes [to the stand], unlocks their umbrella (of

M S V M V O their umbrellaを指す

choice) [by scanning the QR code on its handle] and checks it out

M M V O M

[for as long as they need]. The service is available [for 70 yen] [per

M usersを指す S V C M M

day], [paid via a registered credit card].

分詞構文 M

本文訳

一般的に、日本人は雨が降って濡れるのはあまり好きではない。突然雨が降ると、新しい傘を買う人がたくさんいる。新しく買った傘によくあることだが、最後はさまざまな場所に放置される。日本では年間1億2千万～1億3千万本の傘が販売されているが、日本洋傘振興協議会やその他の資料によると、毎年およそ8,000万本のビニール傘が捨てられている。

ある新興企業が、傘のゴミを減らすのに「*IoT」技術を用いて、東京を中心とした傘の共有サービスをスタートするのに成功した。その企業は2018年12月にそのサービスを始めて、すべてレンタルの傘の利用を目標としている。そのサービスは、「カサ」が傘を意味する日本語なので、アイカサと呼ばれる。

そのサービスの利用者は、LINEのメッセージアプリを経由してその会社に登録し、自分たちの場所に最も近い傘置き場を調べる。利用者はその傘置き場に行き、その取っ手のQRコードを読み取り、選んだ傘のカギを外して、必要な時間それを借り出す。そのサービスは1日70円で利用できて、登録したクレジットカードで支払いをする。

*「IoT」とは、Internet of Thingsの略。あらゆる物がインターネットを通じてつながることで実現するサービスなどのこと。

語彙リスト

□	generally speaking	熟 一般的に言うと
□	wet	形 濡れた
□	as is often the case with	熟 ～にはよくあることだが
□	end up doing	熟 最後は～することになる
□	per	前 ～につき
□	approximately	副 およそ
□	discard	動 捨てる
□	annually	副 毎年
□	source	名 資料
□	start-up company	名 新興企業
□	successfully	副 うまく
□	launch	動 スタートする
□	waste	名 廃棄物
□	aim for	熟 ～を目標とする
□	register	動 登録する
□	via	前 ～経由で
□	location	名 場所
□	unlock	動 カギを外す
□	scan	動 読み取る
□	check out	熟 借り出す
□	as long as	熟 ～の間
□	available	形 利用できる

▶単語10回CHECK 1 □ 2 □ 3 □ 4 □ 5 □ 6 □ 7 □ 8 □ 9 □ 10 □

構文図解

The iKasa system has achieved a 100 percent return rate (of rented umbrellas), [since the registration of credit card numbers connects the umbrellas to the personal information of users]. The Tokyo-based company has installed iKasa spots [at 100 stores, offices and other places] (that have formed partnerships with it).

S: The iKasa system / V: has achieved / O: a 100 percent return rate / M: (of rented umbrellas) / M: [since the registration ... of users]
since：理由のsince「〜ので」
to：connect A to Bのto
S: The Tokyo-based company / V: has installed / O: iKasa spots / M: [at 100 stores, offices and other places] / M: (that have formed partnerships with it)
and：100 stores, offices, other placesの接続
that：関係代名詞のthat
it：The Tokyo-based companyを指す

(A range of) organizations have previously failed [in umbrella-sharing programs] [due to low return rates]. [For example], the Hakodate Chamber of Commerce and Industry and other organizations (in Hakodate, Hokkaido), made 2,300 umbrellas available [for free use] [by tourists], [when the Hokkaido Shinkansen line started in March 2016]. The tourism promotion program ended a year later [because few of the umbrellas had been returned]. A similar program was introduced [by the Shibuya Ward in Tokyo] [about ten years ago], but it failed to last [for the same reason].

M: (A range of) / S: organizations / V: have previously failed / M: [in umbrella-sharing programs] / M: [due to low return rates]
M: [For example] / S: the Hakodate Chamber of Commerce and Industry and other organizations / M: (in Hakodate, Hokkaido) / V: made / O: 2,300 umbrellas / C: available / M: [for free use] / M: [by tourists] / M: [when the Hokkaido Shinkansen line started in March 2016]
S: The tourism promotion program / V: ended / M: a year later / M: [because few of the umbrellas had been returned]
S: A similar program / V: was introduced / M: [by the Shibuya Ward in Tokyo] / M: [about ten years ago] / S: it / V: failed to last / M: [for the same reason]
it：a similar programを指す

The iKasa service has overcome the problem (of people not returning) [because it addresses the issue as "a business]." The founder (of the company) said, "We hope to operate across Japan as an infrastructure such as Japan's excellent railway network."

S: The iKasa service / V: has overcome / O: the problem / M: (of people not returning) / M: [because it addresses the issue as "a business]
people：動名詞の主語
returning：動名詞
it：The iKasa serviceを指す
S: The founder / M: (of the company) / V: said / O: "We hope to operate across Japan as an infrastructure such as Japan's excellent railway network."
to operate：不定詞 名詞的用法

本文訳

アイカサのシステムは、クレジットカード番号の登録が傘と利用者の個人情報を結び付けることになって、レンタルされた傘の100％の返却率を達成した。東京を拠点とする会社は、業務提携した100の店、会社、その他の場所に、アイカサのスタンドを設置した。

さまざまな組織が、以前は低い返却率のせいで、傘の共有事業に失敗してきた。例えば、北海道新幹線が2016年の3月に開通した時に、北海道の函館商工会議所や他の組織が、2,300本の傘を、観光客が無料で使用できるようにした。傘のほとんどが返却されなかったので、その観光プロモーション事業は、1年後に終わった。同様の事業は10年前に東京の渋谷区でも導入されたが、同じ理由で続かなかった。

アイカサのサービスは、その問題に「ビジネス」として取り組むことで、利用者が傘を返却しない問題を克服した。その企業の創業者は、「私たちは日本のすぐれた鉄道網のようなインフラとして、日本中で事業を展開したい」と言った。

語彙リスト

□	return rate	名 返却率
□	registration	名 登録
□	connect A to B	熟 AをBと結び付ける
□	install	動 設置する
□	form	動 形成する
□	a range of	熟 さまざまな～
□	organization	名 組織
□	previously	副 以前
□	fail in	熟 ～で失敗する
□	free	形 無料の
□	tourism	名 観光業
□	promotion	名 プロモーション
□	similar	形 似たような
□	introduce	動 導入する
□	last	動 続く
□	overcome	動 克服する
□	address	動 取り組む
□	issue	名 問題
□	founder	名 創設者
□	operate	動 事業を行う
□	infrastructure	名 インフラ
□	excellent	形 すぐれた
□	railway	名 鉄道

▸単語10回CHECK 1 □ 2 □ 3 □ 4 □ 5 □ 6 □ 7 □ 8 □ 9 □ 10 □

構文図解

Other companies are also addressing the waste (of umbrellas). A soft drink maker (based in the city of Osaka) places free-use umbrellas [next to its vending machines, mainly in office buildings and shopping streets], [because many people notice them and often return to such locations]. Umbrellas (used by this service) include those (provided by railways) (which were left behind on trains and in stations). The corporation started the service [in Osaka] [in 2015] and has since expanded it [to Tokyo and 15 prefectures].

S: Other companies / V: are also addressing / O: the waste / M: (of umbrellas)
S: A soft drink maker / (based in the city of Osaka): 過去分詞の後置修飾 / V: places / O: free-use umbrellas / M: [next to its vending machines, mainly in office buildings and shopping streets]: オフィスビルやショッピングストリートの自動販売機の隣 / M: [because many people notice them and often return to such locations]
them: free-use umbrellas を指す / such locations: umbrellas を指す
S: Umbrellas / M: (used by this service): 過去分詞の後置修飾 / V: include / O: those / M: (provided by railways): 過去分詞の後置修飾 / M: (which were left behind on trains and in stations): 関係代名詞（先行詞は those）
S: The corporation / V: started / O: the service / M: [in Osaka] / M: [in 2015] / V: has since expanded / O: it (the service を指す) / M: [to Tokyo and 15 prefectures]

[In a related development], another company plans ⟨to shortly begin a sharing program at Tokyo-area train stations on a trial basis⟩, [using umbrellas made of Limex, an innovative material it developed from limestone]. The Tokyo-based venture company said ⟨it developed the new material in line with global trends toward reducing plastic use for environmental protection⟩.

M: [In a related development] / S: another company / V: plans / O: ⟨to shortly begin a sharing program at Tokyo-area train stations on a trial basis⟩: 不定詞 名詞的用法
M: [using umbrellas made of Limex, an innovative material it developed from limestone]: 分詞構文 / made: 過去分詞の名詞修飾 / , : 同格のカンマ「すなわち」 / material ▼ it: 関係詞の省略 / it: another company を指す
S: The Tokyo-based venture company / V: said / O: ⟨it developed the new material in line with global trends toward reducing plastic use for environmental protection⟩: 名詞節の that の省略 / it: The Tokyo-based venture company を指す

[As umbrella users], we need to consider not only convenience, but also ⟨how to reduce waste in our societies⟩. [That way], we can comfortably stay dry [on a rainy day] [without hurting our environment].

M: [As umbrella users] / S: we / V: need to consider / O: not only convenience, but also ⟨how to reduce waste in our societies⟩: not only A but also B / how to: 「～する方法」
M: [That way] / S: we / V: can comfortably stay / C: dry / M: [on a rainy day] / M: [without hurting our environment]

本文訳

他の企業も、傘のゴミ問題に取り組んでいる。大阪市に拠点を置くソフトドリンクメーカーは、オフィスビルやショッピングストリートを中心に、自動販売機の隣に無料使用できる傘を設置している。なぜなら多くの人の目に留(と)まり、その場所に返却してくれることが多いからだ。このサービスで使用する傘には、鉄道会社が提供する、電車や駅に置き忘れたものがある。その企業は2015年に大阪でそのサービスを始めて、それ以来、東京など15の都道府県にそのサービスを広げてきた。

関連する開発では、別の企業が、ライメックスという石灰岩から開発された革新的な素材で作られた傘を利用して、東京周辺の電車の駅で、まもなく共有サービスを試験的に開始する予定である。東京に拠点を置くそのベンチャー企業は、環境保護のためにプラスチックの使用を減らす世界的な傾向に合わせて、その新しい素材を開発したと述べた。

傘の利用者として、私たちは利便性だけではなく、社会のゴミを減らす方法を考慮する必要がある。そうすれば、私たちは環境にダメージを与えずに、雨の日も快適に濡れずにいられるのである。

語彙リスト

be based in	熟	～に本拠地がある
vending machine	名	自動販売機
include	動	含む
provide	動	提供する
corporation	名	企業
expand	動	広げる
prefecture	名	県（都道府県）
related	形	関連する
development	名	開発
plan to do	熟	～する予定である
on a ～ basis	熟	～基準で
trial	形	試験的な
innovative	形	革新的な
material	名	素材
limestone	名	石灰岩
in line with	熟	～に合わせて
trend	名	傾向
protection	名	保護
convenience	名	利便性
comfortably	副	快適に
hurt	動	傷つける

▸単語10回CHECK 1 2 3 4 5 6 7 8 9 10

Generally speaking, Japanese people do not really like to get wet when it rains. Many people buy new umbrellas when it suddenly rains. As is often the case with the newly bought ones, they end up being left in various places. While 120 to 130 million umbrellas are sold per year in Japan, approximately 80 million plastic ones are discarded annually, according to the Japan Umbrella Promotion Association and other sources.

A start-up company has successfully launched an umbrella-sharing service, mainly in Tokyo, using "Internet of Things" (IoT) technology to reduce umbrella waste. The company started the service in December 2018, and it aims for the use of all rented umbrellas. The service is called iKasa since "Kasa" is Japanese for umbrella.

Users of the service register with the company via the LINE messaging app and check for the umbrella spots closest to their location. The user goes to the stand, unlocks their umbrella of choice by scanning the QR code on its handle and checks it out for as long as they need. The service is available for 70 yen per day, paid via a registered credit card.

The iKasa system has achieved a 100 percent return rate of rented umbrellas, since the registration of credit card numbers connects the umbrellas to the personal information of users. The Tokyo-based company has installed iKasa spots at 100 stores, offices and other places that have formed partnerships with it.

A range of organizations have previously failed in umbrella-sharing programs due to low return rates. For example, the Hakodate Chamber of Commerce and Industry and other organizations in Hakodate, Hokkaido, made 2,300 umbrellas available for free use by tourists, when the Hokkaido Shinkansen line started in March 2016. The tourism promotion program ended a year later because few of the umbrellas had been returned. A similar program was introduced by the Shibuya Ward in Tokyo about ten years ago, but it failed to last for the same reason.

The iKasa service has overcome the problem of people not

returning because it addresses the issue as "a business." The founder of the company said, "We hope to operate across Japan as an infrastructure such as Japan's excellent railway network."

Other companies are also addressing the waste of umbrellas. A soft drink maker based in the city of Osaka places free-use umbrellas next to its vending machines, mainly in office buildings and shopping streets, because many people notice them and often return to such locations. Umbrellas used by this service include those provided by railways which were left behind on trains and in stations. The corporation started the service in Osaka in 2015 and has since expanded it to Tokyo and 15 prefectures.

In a related development, another company plans to shortly begin a sharing program at Tokyo-area train stations on a trial basis, using umbrellas made of Limex, an innovative material it developed from limestone. The Tokyo-based venture company said it developed the new material in line with global trends toward reducing plastic use for environmental protection.

As umbrella users, we need to consider not only convenience, but also how to reduce waste in our societies. That way, we can comfortably stay dry on a rainy day without hurting our environment.

▸音読10回CHECK 1 ☐ 2 ☐ 3 ☐ 4 ☐ 5 ☐ 6 ☐ 7 ☐ 8 ☐ 9 ☐ 10 ☐

背景知識が広がるコラム

BACKGROUND KNOWLEDGE

sharing economy

本問では、現在流行の*sharing economy*を傘にも適用することで、傘のゴミを減らす方法が挙げられていました。*sharing economy*とは、日本語では「**共有経済**」と言って、インターネットを介して、個人同士でさまざまなものを取り引き、共有するサービスのことです。事業者は、そのプラットフォームを提供する仕組みです。傘の提供も企業が行うことから、個人の所有物を共有するシェアリングエコノミーとは異なりますが、モノを共有するという概念は共通しています。

シェアリングエコノミーの代表例と言えば、2000年代後半からアメリカの西海岸で始まった **Airbnb を筆頭とする民泊**が挙げられるでしょう。民泊とは、**自宅の空き部屋を観光客に安価で貸し出すことで、空き部屋や空き家の有効活用と、宿泊費を安くしたい観光客の両方のニーズを満たすサービス**です。

民泊は主に空間のシェアですが、モノのシェアもあります。例えば、*ridesharing*と呼ばれる、アメリカ発のUberに代表される**自家用車を利用した配車サービス**があります。利用者が、スマートフォンのアプリを使って、近くにいる他人の車に乗るサービスです。タクシーと違って、一般人が自家用車で配車サービスを行う点が最大の特徴です。

その他にも、メルカリに代表される**フリーマーケット**という、**個人の所有するモノを安価に簡単に売買できるサービス**があります。**支払いトラブルを回避する独自の決済方法**や**匿名配送**といった利用者が安心して使えるシステムが高く評価され、急成長を遂げています。

問題 **8**

文 化

男女の性差

別冊 p.34 ／制限時間 25 分／ 583 words

解答

A. ロ　**B.** ハ　**C.** stereotypes　**D.** ハ

E. ロ　**F.** イ　**G.** ハ

H. 女の子が男の子とちょうど同じくらい上手に力強く競技することができると、男の子が理解することは健全だ

I. ロ、ホ

解説

A.

（イ）これは愚かと言ってもいいくらいだ。

（ロ）これは極めて愚かだ。

（ハ）これは決して愚かではない。

（ニ）これは愚かではない。

下線部(1)は**This is beyond stupid**.「**これは愚かを通り越している**」という表現。後ろでこの発言者がpromising never to shop at Target「二度とターゲット社で買い物をしないと誓って」から、「**愚かを通り越してあきれる**」の意味とわかるので、**(ロ) This is extremely stupid.** が正解。Thisは前文の「ターゲット社が、男の子用、女の子用のおもちゃという標示を使うのをやめる」ことを指している。

B.

（イ）それらの意見を持っているたくさんの人が、その批判に抗（あらが）うために集まった。

（ロ）それらの意見を持っているたくさんの人が、その意見を支持するために集まった。

（ハ）それらの意見はたくさんの人に反対された。

（ニ）それらの意見はたくさんの人に支持された。

下線部(2)は、**those voices met a great deal of resistance「そうした声は多くの抵抗にあった」**から、**抵抗とは意見に対する反対のこと**なので、**(ハ) Those opinions were opposed by a lot of people.**が正解。meetの語法に着目する。

語彙 POINT ❺ meetの語法

(例文)
The company will be able to **meet your requirements**.
訳 その会社はあなたの要求を満たしてくれるだろう。

My suggestion **met with** his opposition.
訳 私の提案は彼の反対にあった。

meetの語法でよく狙われるのは、**meet one's requirements (needs, demands)「~の要求を満たす」**です。ここでのmeetは**satisfy「満たす」**と同じ意味なので注意しましょう。続いて**meet with「~に遭遇する・~を受ける」**です。**事故や困難・非難**などをよく目的語にとります。問題文中の下線部(2)のように、withが欠けて直接目的語をとることもあるので、覚えておきましょう。

C.

下線部(3)を含む文は、**children will be happier if they're not forced into (3) boxes according to their sexes「子供は性別に応じた箱に押し込まれないほうが幸せになるだろう」**から、ここでの「箱」**とは性別への固定観念や偏見を意味する**とわかるので、**第4段落最終文**の**stereotypes**が正解。

D.

(イ) 相違点はあるがほとんど類似点はない
(ロ) 類似点よりも相違点のほうが多い
(ハ) 相違点よりも類似点のほうが多い
(ニ) 類似点はなく、相違点だけがある

空欄(X)が含まれているのは、There are (　X　) between males and females「男女間に(　X　)が存在する」という文。**第3段落第4**

文～, women proved that they could do jobs traditionally done by males, like working in factories, while their kids played with toys designed for both girls and boys.「～、女性は工場労働のような男性が従来行ってきた仕事もできると証明したし、一方で、子供は女の子、男の子両方に設計されたおもちゃで遊んだ」から、**男女の類似点を述べている**ので、**(ハ) more similarities than differencesが正解**とわかる。

E.

(イ) きっぱりと終わった　(ロ) すぐに人気になった
(ハ) 完全な災害となった　(ニ) 突然拒絶された

下線部(4)が含まれているのは、**the era of "blue for boys, pink for girls" (4) exploded「『男の子にはブルー、女の子にはピンク』の時代が突然到来した」**という文。この前文では「**2つの別のおもちゃの市場を作ることで、もっとお金を稼ぐことができるとわかった**」とある。性別で色やおもちゃを使い分ける市場が**流行した**という意味だとわかるので、**(ロ) quickly became popularが正解**。

F.

(イ) めったに～ない　(ロ) 時々
(ハ) 親切に　(ニ) すすんで

空所(Y)を含む文は、**Today's men, many of whom were raised to play with toy soldiers rather than baby dolls, still (Y) pursue careers in nursing or child care.「今日の男性の多くは、赤ん坊の人形よりおもちゃの兵隊で遊ぶように育てられたので、看護や育児の世界でキャリアを求めることが、いまだに(Y)」**となる。**おもちゃの兵隊と、看護や育児の世界は遠く離れているので、(イ) rarelyが正解。**

語彙 POINT ❻ **準否定語**

rarely (seldom)「めったに～ない」は**準否定語**と言われて、**notと同様に否定文を作る**ので注意しましょう。**頻度を打ち消す表現**です。他にも、**hardly (scarcely)「ほとんど～ない」**と**程度を打ち消す準否定語**があります。**few, little**は**「ほとんど～ない」**と**数量を打ち消す準否定語**なので注意しましょう。

G.

（イ） 私たちが大人になると、遊びは仕事に取って代わられる。

（ロ） 遊びによって、大人は本当に重要なものから気がそれることがある。

（ハ） 遊びによって、私たちは大人になるとどうなるのかを知ることができる。

（二） 私たちは大人になってもまだ、遊びを通じて価値あるものを学ぶことができる。

下線部(5) play is a way to learn about who we become as adultsは、playがS、isがV、a wayがCの第2文型の文。**to learnは不定詞の形容詞的用法**で、**a way to learn「～を学ぶ方法」**となる。**who we become as adults**は、**whoが疑問詞**で**「どんな人に～か」**、**asは時のas**で、**「大人になった時に私たちはどんな人になるか」**となる。

よって、**(ハ) Play can help us know what we will be like when we become adults.**が正解。**前置詞のlike**を使った**what we will be like「私たちがどのようなものになるか」**の表現に注意する。

H.

構文図解

It's healthy for boys 〈to understand that girls can play just as skillfully and with just as much strength as the boys do〉

It's：S V（形式主語）／healthy：C／for boys：不定詞の主語／to understand ～：S′／that：名詞節のthat／do：playの代動詞

Itは**形式主語のit**で、to understand以下を指す。It is healthyの第2文型の文。

for boysが不定詞の主語、to understandが不定詞の名詞的用法で**「男の子たちが～を理解すること」**の意味。thatは名詞節のthatでdoまでの意味のカタマリを作る。**andはjust as skillfullyとwith just as much strengthを接続**する。ここでのwithは、**with strength**で、**with ＋ 抽象名詞 ＝ 副詞**というルールから、**strongly「強く」**の意味。最後のasは、2つのjust asを受けるasで、**just as ～ as ...「…とちょうど同じくらい～」**となる。以上をまとめると、**「女の子が男の子とちょうど同じくらい上手に力強く競技することができると、男の子が理解することは健全だ」**となる。前後の文脈から、この文の**play**は**「競技する」**の意味。

語彙 POINT ❼ with ＋ 抽象名詞 ＝ 副詞

with ＋ 抽象名詞は1語で**副詞**に置き換えることができます。これがわかると、withのさまざまな用法に迷わずに、正確な意味を理解できるようになります。以下に頻出の表現をまとめます。
with care = carefully「注意深く」／**with ease = easily「簡単に」**
with fluency = fluently「流暢に」

1.

（イ） ターゲット社は、男の子と女の子を異なる売り場へ行くように指示する標示を一度も使ったことがない。

（ロ） 子供は、自分の興味がどこにあるかを確かめるのに、いろいろなおもちゃを試してみる生まれつきの傾向がある。

（ハ） ピンクは、今では特に女の子のための色とみなされているが、かつては男の子に不運なものと信じられていた。

（ニ） 今では、女性が一定の基準を満たす限り、陸軍のどのポストでも任命される可能性がある。

（ホ） 性の不平等を克服するために、男女間のギャップを強調することが必要なことは多い。

（ヘ） 今では、アメリカのほとんどすべての州に、全員が女性のタックル・フットボールのリーグがある。

（ト） 今では、シアトル以外の都市では、男女共用の個室のトイレを見ることができない。

(ロ)は、**第2段落第3文It's natural for kids to experiment with different toys and identities.「子供がいろいろなおもちゃや自分を試すのは自然なことだ」**と一致するので正解。(ホ)は、**第6段落第2文～, fighting for equality often means highlighting gaps between the sexes, ...「～、平等を求めて戦うことは、性別間のギャップを強調するのを意味することが多い、…」**と一致するので正解。

不正解の選択肢を見ていくと、(イ)は、**第1段落第1文～ its stores would stop using signs that ～**から、**今まで使っていた標示(男の子はあるオモチャを買って、女の子は別のおもちゃを買うように促す標示)の使用をやめる**ということなので、不適。

(ハ)は、**第3段落第3文～, pink — now a color closely associated with girls — was considered a color more appropriate for boys.「～、現在では女の子を密接に連想させるピンクは、男の子により適した色だと考えられていた」**と反するので不適。

(ニ)は、**第5段落第2文Today's women, ～, are still excluded from roughly 177,000 posts in the Army, ...「今日の女性は、～、陸軍のおよそ17万7千のポストから、いまだに除外されている」**に反するので、不適。

(ヘ)は、**最終段落第2文Recently, organizers in Utah launched what's believed to be the first all-girls tackle-football league, ～「最近、ユタ州の主催者が、初めての女性だけのタックルフットボールリーグになると考えられているものをスタートして」に反する**ので不適。**本文は「ユタ州」で、選択肢(ヘ)の「アメリカのほぼすべての州」という表記はない**ので不適。解法 POINT ❸ **(p.59)** で学んだように、**言い過ぎの選択肢**に注意する。

(ト)は、**最終段落第4文～, Seattle became the third city to make it a rule that all single-stall bathrooms be labeled unisex.「シアトルは、すべての独立型の公共のトイレのすべてにユニセックスの標示をすることを法制化した3番目の都市になった」**に反するので不適。**make it a rule that ～「～を決まりとする」**は、**make O C**のOに**形式目的語のit**が使われていることに注意する。

構文図解

[When Target, a giant discount chain in the US, announced that its stores would stop using signs that directed boys to buy certain toys (such as trucks and toy soldiers) and girls to buy others (such as dolls and pretty costumes)], hundreds visited its website [to complain]. "This is beyond stupid," wrote one customer, [promising never to shop at Target]. "Boys will always be boys and girls will always be girls!" said another.

同格のカンマ　M　名詞節のthat　関係代名詞のthat　boys to ～とgirls to ～の接続　ターゲット社が男の子用のおもちゃと女の子用のおもちゃの標示をやめたこと　S　V　O　不定詞 副詞的用法　M　O　V　S　分詞構文　M　O　習性のwill

But those voices met (a great deal of) resistance. Many parents and commenters expressed support [after the announcement], no doubt [because they've started to realize something psychologists have been saying for years]: 〈that children will be happier if they're not forced into boxes according to their sexes〉. It's natural for kids 〈to experiment with different toys and identities〉. Dismissing such tendencies "can limit how kids view themselves, what skills they develop, and what their interests become," says Debbie Sterling, founder of Goldie Blox, which makes construction toys [for girls].

男の子には男の子のおもちゃを、女の子には女の子のおもちゃを与えるべきだという声　S　V　M　O　S　V　O　不定詞 名詞的用法　M　M　M　関係詞の省略　名詞節のthat　O　childrenを指す　形式主語のit　S　V　C　不定詞の主語　不定詞 名詞的用法　S′　動名詞　O　「どのように～か」　「どんな名詞を～か」　「何に～か」　V　S　同格のカンマ　S′　V　O　M

It's also an urge (driven in large part by marketing). "There are more similarities than differences between males and females," says Stephanie Coontz, an author and historian.

性別でおもちゃを分けないこと　S　V　M　C　過去分詞の名詞修飾　M　O　more A than B「BというよりむしろA」　V　S　同格のカンマ　S′

本文訳

アメリカの巨大ディスカウントチェーンであるターゲット社が、各店舗では、男の子にはトラックやおもちゃの兵隊のような特定のおもちゃを買うように、女の子には人形やかわいい衣装などのおもちゃを買うように促す標示を使うのをやめると発表したとき、何百人もの人が抗議をしに、そのウェブサイトを訪れた。「これはあきれてものが言えない」と、ある顧客は書き込みをして、二度とターゲット社で買い物をしないと誓った。また別の顧客は、「男の子はいつも男の子だし、女の子はいつも女の子だ！」と言った。

しかし、そうした声はかなりの抵抗にあった。多くの親やコメント投稿者が、その発表後に支持を表明した理由は、間違いなく心理学者が長年言い続けたことを認識し始めたからだった。すなわち、子供は性別に応じた箱に押し込まれないほうが幸せになるだろうということだ。子供がいろいろなおもちゃや自分を試すのは自然なことだ。そのような傾向を無視することは、「子供が自分をどう見るか、どんな技術を磨くか、そして彼らの興味がどうなるかを制限する可能性がある」と、女の子にブロックのおもちゃを製造するゴールディーブロックス社の創業者であるデビー・スターリングは言う。

それはまた、大部分が市場により動かされた衝動だ。「男性と女性には違いよりも類似点のほうが多い」と作家で歴史家のステファニー・クーンツは言う。

語彙リスト

giant	形	巨大な
discount	名	割引
announce	動	公表する
sign	名	標示
direct O to do	熟	Oを～するように促す
certain	形	特定の
complain	動	不平を言う
customer	名	顧客
promise to do	動	～することを約束する
meet	動	～にあう
a great deal of	熟	大量の
resistance	名	抵抗
commenter	名	コメントを投稿する人
support	名	支持
no doubt	熟	間違いなく
psychologist	名	心理学者
force O into	熟	Oを～に押し込む
sex	名	性別
experiment with	熟	～を試す
dismiss	動	無視する
tendency	名	傾向
limit	動	制限する
view	動	見る
founder	名	創業者
construction toy	名	ブロックのおもちゃ
urge	名	衝動
similarity	名	類似点
author	名	作家

▸単語10回CHECK 1 2 3 4 5 6 7 8 9 10

構文図解

[In the early 20th century], [for example], pink — now a color closely associated with girls — was considered a color (more appropriate for boys). During World War II, Coontz notes, women proved that they could do jobs traditionally done by males, like working in factories, while their kids played with toys designed for both girls and boys.

M M S S′ 過去分詞の名詞修飾 V C M 形容詞の後置修飾 O S V O 名詞節のthat 過去分詞の後置修飾 前置詞のlike 過去分詞の後置修飾

But [by the 1980s], toy companies (like Mattel and Hasbro) had figured out 〈that they could make more money by creating two separate toy markets〉. And so the era (of "blue for boys, pink for girls)" exploded; [along with it] came many new stereotypes (about what we should like and how we should be).

M S 前置詞のlike M V 名詞節のthat toy companiesを指す O 「男の子に青、女の子にピンクの時代が到来したこと」 S M V M V S M 「何を～か」 「どのように～か」

These expectations continue well [beyond childhood]. Today's women, (who grew up at a time when girls were not encouraged to pick up toy soldiers), are still excluded [from roughly 177,000 posts in the Army], a branch of the military that separated sexes until nearly 1980. Today's men, (many of whom were raised to play with toy soldiers rather than baby dolls), still rarely pursue careers [in nursing or child care].

S 自分の理想像への新しい固定観念 V M M S M 関係副詞 V M 同格のカンマ M′ 関係代名詞のthat S M 不定詞 副詞的用法 M M V O M

現代女性の多くが陸軍の要職から除外されていることや現代男性の多くが看護・育児職に就かないこと

[Of course], none (of this) means 〈that there are no differences between men and women or that emphasizing them can't be helpful〉.

M S M V 名詞節のthat O 名詞節のthat differences between men and womenを指す

本文訳

例えば、現在では女の子を密接に連想させる色のピンクは、20世紀初頭では、男の子により適した色だと考えられていた。第二次世界大戦中、女性は工場労働のような男性が従来行ってきた仕事もできると証明したし、一方で、子供は女の子、男の子両方に設計されたおもちゃで遊んだことにクーンツは注目する。

しかし1980年代までに、マテル社、ハズブロ社のような玩具(がんぐ)メーカーは、2つの別のおもちゃ市場を作ることで、もっとお金を稼ぐことができるとわかった。そして、「男の子にはブルー、女の子にはピンク」の時代が突然到来した。それとともに、私たちが何を好み、どうあるべきかに関する多くの新しい固定観念が生まれた。

こうした期待は、子供時代をはるかに越えて続く。今日の女性は、女の子がおもちゃの兵隊を選ぶようには促されなかった時代に成長して、ほぼ1980年までずっと男女を区別していた軍の支部である陸軍の、およそ17万7千のポストから、いまだに除外されている。今日の男性の多くは、赤ん坊の人形よりおもちゃの兵隊で遊ぶように育てられたので、看護や育児の世界でキャリアを求めることは、いまだにめったにない。

もちろん、このどれもが、男性と女性に違いがまったくないとか、男女の違いを強調しても役に立たないということを意味するわけではない。

語彙リスト

closely	副 密接に
be associated with	熟 ～を連想する
appropriate	形 適切な
note	動 注目する
traditionally	副 従来
design	動 設計する
figure out	熟 ～を理解する
separate	形 別々の
era	名 時代
explode	動 突然現れる
along with	熟 ～と一緒に
stereotype	名 固定観念
expectation	名 期待
encourage O to do	熟 Oに～するように促す
pick up	熟 選ぶ
exclude	動 除外する
roughly	副 だいたい
branch	名 支部
military	名 軍
nearly	副 ほぼ
raise	動 育てる
B rather than A	熟 AよりむしろB
rarely	副 めったに～ない
pursue	動 追求する
nursing	名 看護
child care	名 育児
emphasize	動 強調する
helpful	形 役に立つ

▸単語10回CHECK 1 2 3 4 5 6 7 8 9 10

構文図解

[For instance], 〈fighting for equality〉 often means 〈highlighting
M　動名詞　S　M　V　動名詞　O

gaps between the sexes, especially in areas like economic status〉.
前置詞のlike

"But play is a way to learn about who we become as adults," says
O　不定詞　形容詞的用法　「どんな人に～か」　V

Ellen Dubois, who teaches history and gender [at an American
S　V　O　M

university]. "Toys and what they signify, (which is the free
S　関係代名詞　toysを指す　M

expression of play among children), should be as open and diverse
V　C

as～as possible「できる限り～」
[as possible]."
M

[Beyond Target's decision], there are signs 〈that we, as a society,
M　M　V　S　同格のthat　M

are starting to accept more flexible gender roles〉. Recently,
不定詞　名詞的用法　M

organizers (in Utah) launched 〈what's believed to be the first all-
S　M　V　関係代名詞のwhat　O

girls tackle-football league〉, and advocates are pushing for more
S　V　O

mixed-sex sports [for pre-teenage children]. "It's healthy for boys to
M　形式主語　不定詞の主語

understand that girls can play just as skillfully and with just as
不定詞　名詞的用法　名詞節のthat　O

much strength as the boys do," says Nancy Hogshead-Makar, a
playの代動詞　V　S　同格のカンマ

former Olympic swimmer. [Not long ago], Seattle became the third city
S′　形式目的語　M　S　V　C

(to make it a rule that all single-stall bathrooms be labeled unisex).
不定詞　形容詞的用法　M　名詞節のthat

The move was driven [by people who often say they feel unwelcome
S　V　M　名詞節のthatの省略　peopleを指す

in the men's room and the women's room — and who, as kids, were

likely to feel as if they were forced into the wrong toy section].
kidsを指す

本文訳

例えば、平等を求めて戦うことは、特に経済的地位のような分野で性別間のギャップを強調することが多くなる。「しかし、遊びは大人になったときどんな人になるかに関して学ぶ方法だ」と、アメリカン大学で歴史と*ジェンダー論を教えるエレン・デュボイスは言う。「おもちゃやそれが意味するものは、子供が自由に遊びを表現できるもので、できる限りオープンで多様であるべきだ」。

ターゲット社の決定以外にも、私たちは社会全体で、もっと柔軟な性別の役割を受け入れ始めている兆しがある。最近、ユタ州の主催者が、初めてと思われる女性だけのタックルフットボールリーグをスタートしており、支持者は、10代になる前の子供のために男女両方で行うスポーツを強く求めている。「男の子が、女の子も自分たちとちょうど同じくらい上手に、力強く競技することができると理解することは健全だ」と、以前オリンピックに出場したことのある水泳選手であるナンシー・ホグスヘッドは言う。それほど昔のことではないが、シアトルは、すべての個室型の公共のトイレに*ユニセックスの表示をすることを法制化した3番目の都市になった。その動きは、男性用のトイレや女性用のトイレでは入りにくいと感じるとよく言う人によって推進されたが、そのような人は、子供のころ、無理やり好みとは違うおもちゃ売り場に行かされたように感じていたことだろう。

*「ジェンダー論」は、歴史的、社会的に作られた男女の差異を研究する学問のこと。
*「ユニセックス」は、男女の区別がないこと。

語彙リスト

単語	品詞	意味
equality	名	平等
highlight	動	強調する
economic	形	経済の
status	名	地位
gender	名	ジェンダー、性別
signify	動	意味する
diverse	形	多様な
decision	名	決定
flexible	形	柔軟な
organizer	名	主催者
launch	動	開始する

単語	品詞	意味
advocate	名	支持者
push for	熟	～を強く要求する
skillfully	副	上手に
strength	名	力
former	形	以前の
stall	名	個室
label O C	動	OにCと表示する
unisex	形	男女共用の
unwelcome	形	歓迎されない
section	名	区画

▸単語10回CHECK 1 2 3 4 5 6 7 8 9 10

When Target, a giant discount chain in the US, announced that its stores would stop using signs that directed boys to buy certain toys (such as trucks and toy soldiers) and girls to buy others (such as dolls and pretty costumes) , hundreds visited its website to complain. "This is beyond stupid," wrote one customer, promising never to shop at Target. "Boys will always be boys and girls will always be girls!" said another.

But those voices met a great deal of resistance. Many parents and commenters expressed support after the announcement, no doubt because they've started to realize something psychologists have been saying for years: that children will be happier if they're not forced into boxes according to their sexes. It's natural for kids to experiment with different toys and identities. Dismissing such tendencies "can limit how kids view themselves, what skills they develop, and what their interests become," says Debbie Sterling, founder of Goldie Blox, which makes construction toys for girls.

It's also an urge driven in large part by marketing. "There are more similarities than differences between males and females," says Stephanie Coontz, an author and historian. In the early 20th century, for example, pink — now a color closely associated with girls — was considered a color more appropriate for boys. During World War II, Coontz notes, women proved that they could do jobs traditionally done by males, like working in factories, while their kids played with toys designed for both girls and boys.

But by the 1980s, toy companies like Mattel and Hasbro had figured out that they could make more money by creating two separate toy markets. And so the era of "blue for boys, pink for girls" exploded; along with it came many new stereotypes about what we should like and how we should be.

These expectations continue well beyond childhood. Today's women, who grew up at a time when girls were not encouraged to pick up toy soldiers, are still excluded from roughly 177,000 posts in the Army, a branch of the military that separated sexes until nearly

1980. Today's men, many of whom were raised to play with toy soldiers rather than baby dolls, still rarely pursue careers in nursing or child care.

Of course, none of this means that there are no differences between men and women or that emphasizing them can't be helpful. For instance, fighting for equality often means highlighting gaps between the sexes, especially in areas like economic status. "But play is a way to learn about who we become as adults," says Ellen Dubois, who teaches history and gender at an American university. "Toys and what they signify, which is the free expression of play among children, should be as open and diverse as possible."

Beyond Target's decision, there are signs that we, as a society, are starting to accept more flexible gender roles. Recently, organizers in Utah launched what's believed to be the first all-girls tackle-football league, and advocates are pushing for more mixed-sex sports for preteenage children. "It's healthy for boys to understand that girls can play just as skillfully and with just as much strength as the boys do," says Nancy Hogshead-Makar, a former Olympic swimmer. Not long ago, Seattle became the third city to make it a rule that all single-stall bathrooms be labeled unisex. The move was driven by people who often say they feel unwelcome in the men's room and the women's room — and who, as kids, were likely to feel as if they were forced into the wrong toy section.

▸音読10回CHECK 1 2 3 4 5 6 7 8 9 10

背景知識が
広がるコラム

BACKGROUND KNOWLEDGE

固定的性別役割分担

私が子供のころは、「**男の子なんだから〜、女の子なんだから〜**」といういわゆる**固定的性別役割分担**が強かったように思います。当たり前のように男の子は青色で、女の子はピンクと受け入れてきました。しかし、本問を読んで、実は社会が作り出した**固定観念**だと知って、少し驚きを覚えました。

子供のころは、「男の子なんだから簡単に泣くな、人前で泣くな」と言われてきました。一方で、「男の子なんだから、女の子には優しくするように、女の子を守ってあげるように」とよい意味での性別役割分担もあった気がします。

男が外で働き、女は家を守るという**固定的性別役割分担**が根強く社会を支配してきました。その役割分担に賛同して受け入れる夫婦はよいのでしょう。しかし、**女性が外で働きたいという肯定的な意思を否定することはあってはならない**ことです。特に、共働きがこれだけ増えてきた現代においては、**労働を男女間でシェアする以上、家事や育児も上手に男女間でシェアすることが大切**なのでしょう。

受け入れられる人にとっては、**固定的性別役割分担**にはよい側面もあるでしょう。しかし、**この概念に苦しむ人がいる以上、そうした弱い立場の人の声に社会全体が耳を傾けて、できる限り改善をはかり、現代社会特有の生きづらさを解消していかなければなりません。**

問題 9

環 境

気候変動とサウンドスケープ

別冊 p.40 ／制限時間 30 分／ 514 words

解答

(1)	ハ	(2)	ハ	(3)	ロ	(4)	ハ	(5)	ハ
(6)	ロ	(7)	ニ	(8)	ロ	(9)	イ	(10)	ハ
(11)	ハ	(12)	ニ	(13)	イ				

解説

(1)

イ．目的　　ロ．歴史　　ハ．影響　　ニ．利用

空欄(a)を含む文は、～, the polar bear in particular has become a powerful symbol of the (a) of climate change.「特にホッキョクグマは、気候変動の(a)の強力な象徴となっている」となる。ホッキョクグマの生息する北極周辺は、地球温暖化のような気候変動の影響をもっとも受けやすいので、「ホッキョクグマは、気候変動の**影響**を受ける代表的な例だ」と推論できる。**ハ. impact** が正解。

(2)

イ．気候変動は、地球規模でさまざまな問題を引き起こしている。

ロ．気候変動のせいで、病気がより広範囲に広がることがある。

ハ．昆虫は水のような資源にマイナスの影響を与えている。

ニ．気候変動の影響は、目に見えるだけではなく聞くこともできる。

Aの内容に合っていないものという指示なので、**NOT 問題と同じ**とみなして、消去法で解答する。イは**段落Aの第2文 It is contributing to an increase in extreme weather「それ（気候変動）が原因で、異常気象が増加している」と合致しているので、不適**。重要な構文なので解説する。

構文 POINT ⑤ contribute toは因果関係を作る

contribute toは直訳だと「**～に貢献する**」ですが、主語と目的語に**因果関係**を作ります。次の例文をご覧ください。
（例文）
Too much salt can **contribute to** high blood pressure.
訳 過度の塩分が原因で、高血圧になる可能性がある。
「貢献する」はプラスの結果をもたらしますが、例文のようにマイナスの結果をもたらす場合は、特に**因果関係を意識して訳出**しましょう。「**Sが原因でOになる**」を基本に訳出しましょう。

ロも**段落Aの第2文 It is contributing to ～ , and a greater number of disease-carrying insects,** から、「**気候変動が原因で、病気を運ぶ虫の数が増える**」と一致するので、不適。ハは本文に記述がないので正解。

ニは**段落Aの最終文However, there is another, often ignored indicator of the health of our planet: its soundscape.**「**しかし、無視されることが多い地球の健康の指標が（目に見える北極圏の影響に加えて）もう1つある。それは、サウンドスケープだ**」とあり、サウンドスケープとは、**鳥や虫の鳴き声で地球の状態をはかる**ものなので、**ニ The effects of climate change can not only be seen but heard.** に一致しているので不適。

(3)
イ. アイデアの詰め合わせ　　ロ. データの集積
ハ. 答えのグループ　　ニ. 議論の種類

下線部①を含む文は、**～, he has created a valuable ①resource for other ecologists to study.**「**彼（クラウス）は、他の生態学者が研究する価値のある資料を作った**」から、**ロ collection of data**が正解。**resource**とは「**情報の供給源**」、つまり「**資料**」のこと。

(4)
イ. ～の自信　　ロ. ～の必要条件
ハ. ～の理解　　ニ. ～に関する心配

解法 POINT ⑤ 英文のパラフレーズに注意する!!

英語の長文では、**抽象的でわかりにくい文**を、次の文で**パラフレーズ**することで、説得力を高めていきます。抽象的な英文が設問になるので、その**次の文がその設問を解き明かすカギを握っている**ことがよくあります。

空欄(b)を含む文は、Natural soundscapes give us information necessary to our (b) the natural world. で、次の文がThey allow us to perceive whether or not an environment is healthy. となる。**Theyは前文の主語のNatural soundscapes**を指すこと、our (b) the natural worldがus to **perceive** whether or not an environment is healthyにパラフレーズされていることに気付くと、**perceive「認識する」**に近い意味の**ハ. understanding of**が正解とわかる。

---

(5)

イ. サウンドスケープを録音するために、クラウスは多くの機器を必要としている。

ロ. クラウスがサウンドスケープ生態学を発見するのに、ほぼ50年かかった。

ハ. クラウスはサウンドスケープが環境の状態を明らかにすると信じている。

ニ. クラウスは、カリフォルニアの森林の木々が作り出した音に集中する。

ハは、**段落B第4文後半Natural soundscapes give us information necessary to our understanding of the natural world.「自然のサウンドスケープによって、私たちは自然界を理解するのに必要な情報を得られる」**と一致。

不正解の選択肢を見ていくと、イは**段落B第2文Using a microphone and a recorder, ~.「マイクや録音機を使って、~」**に不一致。ロは、**同段落第3文In the nearly 50 years Krause has been doing this, he has created a valuable resource for other ecologists to study.「クラウスがこの研究をしてきたほぼ50年で、彼は他の生態学者が研究する価値のある資料を作った」**とあるだけで、サウンドスケープ生態学の発見に50年かかったとは書いていないので不適。

二は、**同段落第2文後半the gurgle of rivers and the melody of birdsong, the humming of insects「川の流れの音、鳥の鳴き声、昆虫の羽音」**から、**木々が作り出した音だけではないので不一致。**

(6)

イ．最終的に　ロ．著しく　ハ．繰り返し　ニ．静かに

下線部②**significantly「著しく」**と同義なのは、**ロ. remarkably**である。形容詞は**remarkable「注目すべき」**で、以下に語源を解説する。

語彙 POINT ❽　markは「印」の意味

remarkableは、**re「何度も」**＋**mark「印」**＋**-able「～できる」**＝「**何度も印をつけることができる**」＝「**注目すべき**」となります。他にも**landmark = land「土地」**＋**mark「印」**＝「**画期的事件**」が同じmarkを使った単語です。元々は「**その土地の目印になるもの**」から、用法が広がって「**その時代の目印になるもの**」＝「**画期的事件**」となりました。

(7)

クラウスが通常の録音場所に戻った時に気付いた、鳥の鳴き声がないことは（　　）。

イ．その環境を多様なものにした
ロ．春に雨がより少ないので起きた
ハ．気候変動を引き起こした
ニ．彼にとっては衝撃的だったが、そんなに驚きではなかった

段落Cの第2文what he heard was shockingと**同段落第5文This was not entirely unexpected「これ（鳥の鳴き声がまったく聞こえなくなっていたこと）はまったく予想外というわけではなかった」**から、**ニ. was shocking but not really surprising to him**が正解。

(8)

イ．価値が下落していること　ロ．音が静かになっていること
ハ．質が向上したこと　ニ．量が少なくなっていること

空欄(c)を含む文は、The（　c　）of these soundscapes is an urgent warning about the effects of climate change.「こうしたサウンドスケープの（　c　）は、気候変動の影響についての緊急の**警告**だ」から、マイナスのニュアンスを持つイ、ロ、ニに正解の候補を絞ることができる。The（　c　）of these soundscapesは前文の**similar changes in the soundscape**を指しているとわかり、さらに同文が**段落Cの最終文後半 the animals that live there are falling silent「そこに生息する動物は静かになりつつある」**から、**ロ. growing silence**が正解とわかる。

(9)

イ. ～の明らかな兆候である　　ロ. ～と反対の主張だ
ハ. ～への答えを確かに提示する　　ニ. 疑いなく予言しようとする

下線部③を含む部分は、the changing soundscapes "③speak strongly to all the climate issues we are now facing「**サウンドスケープが変化しているのは、私たちが現在直面しているあらゆる気候問題に強く語りかけている**」から、「**強く語りかける**」とは、「**サウンドスケープの変化は、～気候問題の明らかな兆候だ**」とわかるので**イ. are a clear sign of** が正解。

(10)

イ. クラウスのサウンドスケープの録音は、あらゆるところで自然の生息地に害を与えてきた。
ロ. 自然のサウンドスケープに貢献する動物が、ますます増えている。
ハ. サウンドスケープが変化することで、私たちは環境が重大な危機にさらされているとわかる。
ニ. 自然の新しい沈黙が、地球の独自性を反映する。

ハは、**段落Dの第3文the changing soundscapes "speak strongly to all the climate issues we are now facing「サウンドスケープが変化しているのは、私たちが現在直面しているあらゆる気候問題に強く語りかけている」**と一致するので正解。

不正解の選択肢を見ていくと、イは本文に記述なし。ロは、**段落Dの最終文More than 50 percent of the thousands of unique habitats captured in his recordings are now almost completely silent, ～.「彼が録音でとった数千の独特の生息地の50%以上が、～、今やほ**

ほ完全に無音で～」に反するので不適。ニは本文に記述なし。

(11)

イ. 応用される　ロ. 許可される
ハ. 押し出される　ニ. 関係している

下線部④を含む文は、**～ in the next 25-30 years, up to one-quarter of the world's species may disappear, ④driven to extinction by climate change.**「～次の25～30年後に、世界の種の4分の1に至るまで、気候変動によって絶滅に**追いやられて**、消滅するかもしれない～」から、「**追いやられる**」に近い意味の**ハ. pushed**が正解。

(12)

イ. ～に例えられる　ロ. ～から落ちる
ハ. ～で留まる　ニ. ～に増加する

空欄(d)を含む文は、That number could (d) an astonishing 50 percent by 2100.「その数字は2100年までには、驚きの50%にまで(d)可能性がある」という文。**That numberは前文のone-quarter、すなわち25%を指す**ので、**25%から50%への推移**は**ニ. rise to**が正解とわかる。

(13)

イ. クラウスの録音は、ある種が存在していた唯一の証拠になるかもしれない。
ロ. より静かなサウンドスケープは、地球規模で種の急速な滅亡につながっている。
ハ. サウンドスケープ生態学者は、私たちがまだ発見していない動物を保護する助けとなる。
ニ. 人類の活動にもかかわらず、サウンドスケープは静かになりつつある。

段落E第3文～ Krause's recordings contain sounds made by undiscovered animals that have now disappeared and will never be known to us.「クラウスの録音に、今は消えて、決して私たちにはわからない未発見の動物が出した音が含まれている～」から、イが正解。ロ、ハ、ニは本文に記述なし。

構文図解

A Climate change is greatly affecting our world. It is contributing to an increase (in extreme weather), more competition (for resources such as water), and (a greater number of) disease-carrying insects, [while at the same time having a negative effect on a wide variety of animals]. These animals range [from sea turtles to pandas to polar bears]. [Struggling to survive as Arctic ice melts due to global warming], the polar bear (in particular) has become a powerful symbol (of the impact of climate change). However, there is another, often ignored indicator (of the health of our planet): its soundscape.

climate change を指す / an increase ～、more competition ～、a greater ～の接続 / it (climate change) is の省略 / 気候変動の影響を受けている動物 / from A to B to C「AからB、Cに至るまで」 / 分詞構文 / 時の as

B Soundscape ecology is the study (of nature's sounds). [Using a microphone and a recorder], American soundscape ecologist Bernie Krause has been recording the sounds (of California's forests) [for many years]: the gurgle of rivers and the melody of birdsong, the humming of insects. [In the nearly 50 years Krause has been doing this], he has created a valuable resource (for other ecologists to study). He believes strongly in the importance (of recording soundscapes), [saying, "Natural soundscapes give us information necessary to our understanding of the natural world]. They allow us to perceive whether or not an environment is healthy."

分詞構文 / サウンドスケープの録音 / 関係詞の省略 / 不定詞 形容詞的用法 / 不定詞の主語 / 分詞構文 / 形容詞の後置修飾 / natural soundscapes を指す / to do / whether or not「～かどうか」

本文訳

A　気候変動は、世界に大きな影響を与えている。気候変動のせいで、異常気象が増えて、水などの資源をめぐる競争、そして病気を*媒介する虫がますます増加している一方で、同時にそれは非常に多くの動物にマイナスの影響を与えている。こうした動物の中には、ウミガメ、パンダ、そしてホッキョクグマなどがいる。地球温暖化が原因で北極の氷が解ける中、生き延びるのに苦労しているので、ホッキョクグマは、特に気候変動の影響の強力なシンボルとなっている。しかし、無視されることが多い地球の健康の指標がもう1つある。それは、サウンドスケープだ。

B　サウンドスケープ生態学とは、自然界の音の研究である。アメリカのサウンドスケープ生態学者のバーニー・クラウスは、マイクやレコーダーを使用して、長年カリフォルニアの森林の音を録音している。川の流れの音、鳥の鳴き声、昆虫の羽音などの録音だ。クラウスがこの研究をしてきたほぼ50年で、彼は他の生態学者が研究する価値のある資料を作った。彼はサウンドスケープを録音することが重要だと強く信じていて、次のように言っている。「自然のサウンドスケープによって、私たちは自然界を理解するのに必要な情報を得られる。そのおかげで、私たちは環境が健全かどうかを認識することができる」。

*「媒介する」は、今まで接点のなかった2つのものの間に立って、何らかの関係をつけること。

語彙リスト

climate change	名	気候変動
affect	動	影響を与える
contribute to	熟	～の一因となる
extreme weather	名	異常気象
competition	名	競争
resource	名	資源、資料
insect	名	昆虫
have an effect on	熟	～に影響を与える
negative	形	否定的な
a wide variety of	熟	非常に多くの種類の
range from A to B	熟	AからBまで及ぶ
polar bear	名	ホッキョクグマ
struggle to do	熟	～するのに苦労する
melt	動	溶ける、解ける
due to	熟	～が原因で
global warming	名	地球温暖化
in particular	熟	特に
symbol	名	象徴
indicator	名	指標
soundscape	名	サウンドスケープ
ecology	名	生態学
gurgle	名	ごぼごぼという音
humming	名	羽音
nearly	副	ほぼ
valuable	形	価値のある
perceive	動	認識する

▸単語10回CHECK 1 2 3 4 5 6 7 8 9 10

構文図解

C Krause's early recordings (in the California forests) were rich and full [of life], a celebration of biodiversity. But [when he returned last spring to his usual recording spot in Sugarloaf Ridge Stat. Park], 〈what he heard〉 was shocking. "The sounds of the forest had changed significantly," Krause says. "It was the first spring in my 77 years that I heard no birdsong at all." This was not entirely unexpected, he explains. California's forests have been severely affected [by years of drought, or lack of rain], [due to climate change]. [As the once-healthy forest habitat is damaged], the animals (that live there) are falling silent.

S M V C / 同格のカンマ M M / 関係代名詞 S V C O / S V / 部分否定 / It is A that ～の強調構文 鳥の鳴き声がまったく聞こえないこと O / S V S V / M 同格の or「すなわち」 M / 理由の as M S / 関係代名詞 M V C

D Sadly, Krause has found similar changes (in the soundscape of natural habitats around the world from the Amazon to Zimbabwe to Borneo). The growing silence (of these soundscapes) is an urgent warning (about the effects of climate change). Krause says 〈the changing soundscapes "speak strongly to all the climate issues we are now facing, from global warming to shifts in the number and variety of bird, frog and mammal populations〉."

M S V O M / from A to B to C「AからB、Cに至るまで」 / S M V C / M S V / 名詞節の that の省略 O / 関係詞の省略 from A to B「AからBまで」 / bird, frog, mammal の接続

本文訳

C　カリフォルニアの森林でのクラウスの初期の録音は、豊かで生命に満ちていて、それは*生物多様性を称(たた)えるものだった。しかし、いつもの録音場所であるシュガーローフ・リッジ州立公園に、昨年の春に戻ってきたとき彼が耳にしたのは、衝撃的なものだった。「森林の音は著しく変わってしまった」とクラウスは言う。「私の77年の人生で初めて、春に鳥の鳴き声をまったく聞かなかった」。これはまったく予想できなかったわけではないと彼は説明する。カリフォルニアの森林は、気候変動による長年の干ばつ、すなわち雨不足により深刻な影響を受けてきた。かつて健全だった森林生息地がダメージを受けているので、そこに生息する動物は静かになりつつある。

D　悲しいことに、クラウスはアマゾン川からジンバブエ、ボルネオに至るまで、世界中の自然の生息地のサウンドスケープが同様に変化していることを発見した。こうしたサウンドスケープがますます静かになっているのは、気候変動の影響についての緊急の警告だ。クラウスは、サウンドスケープが変化しているのは、「地球温暖化から、鳥、カエル、そして哺乳動物の数や種類が変化していることまで、私たちが現在直面しているあらゆる気候問題に強く語りかけている」と言う。

*「生物多様性」は、いろいろな生物が存在している様子。

語彙リスト

□	celebration	名 祝福
□	biodiversity	名 生物多様性
□	spot	名 場所
□	significantly	副 著しく
□	not entirely	熟 まったく~なわけではない
□	severely	副 深刻なほど
□	drought	名 干ばつ
□	habitat	名 生息地
□	fall silent	熟 静かになる
□	urgent	形 緊急の
□	warning	名 警告
□	issue	名 問題
□	shift	名 変化
□	frog	名 カエル
□	mammal	名 哺乳類

▸単語10回CHECK 1 □ 2 □ 3 □ 4 □ 5 □ 6 □ 7 □ 8 □ 9 □ 10 □

構文図解

More than 50 percent (of the thousands of unique habitats captured in his recordings) are now almost completely silent, unrecognizable [because of the damage that humankind has done to the environment].

S: More than 50 percent / M: (of the thousands ... in his recordings) / V: are / M: now / C: almost completely silent / C: unrecognizable / M: [because of ... environment]
captured：過去分詞の後置修飾　that：関係代名詞

E Krause says [of his earlier recordings], "These are soundscapes that no one will hear again in their natural state. They exist today only as a kind of memory, a digital impression of what once existed."

S: Krause / V: says / M: [of his earlier recordings] / O: "These ... existed."
These：クラウスの昔の録音　that：関係代名詞　They：クラウスの昔の録音　what：関係代名詞

It is highly likely 〈that Krause's recordings contain sounds made by undiscovered animals that have now disappeared and will never be known to us〉. Scientists estimate 〈that in the next 25-30 years, up to one-quarter of the world's species may disappear, driven to extinction by climate change〉. That number could rise [to an astonishing 50 percent] [by 2100]. [As Krause puts it], "A great silence is spreading [over the natural world], [at the same time that the sound of humankind is becoming deafening]."

It：形式主語　S: It / V: is / C: highly likely / S′: 〈that ... known to us〉
that：名詞節のthat　made：過去分詞の後置修飾　that：関係代名詞のthat
S: Scientists / V: estimate / O: 〈that ... climate change〉
that：名詞節のthat　driven：分詞構文
That：世界の種の4分の1　S: That number / V: could rise / M: [to an astonishing 50 percent] / M: [by 2100]
M: [As Krause puts it]　As：様態のas　it：主節を指す
S: A great silence / V: is spreading / M: [over the natural world] / M: [at the same time that ... deafening]
at the same time that ～「～と同時に」

本文訳

彼が録音でとった数千もの独特な生息地の50%以上が、人間が環境に与えたダメージが原因で、ほぼ完全に無音で認識できない。
E クラウスは彼の昔の録音について、「これは元の自然の状態では再び聞くことはできないサウンドスケープである。それらは、一種の記憶、つまりかつて存在していたものの、デジタルな痕跡（こんせき）（コンピューター上のデータ）としてしか今日残っていない」と言う。クラウスの録音に、今は消えて、決して私たちには知られていない未発見の動物が出した音が含まれている可能性が非常に高い。科学者は、次の25 ～ 30年後に、世界の種の4分の1に至るまで、気候変動によって絶滅に追いやられて、消滅するかもしれないと推測する。その数字は、2100年までに、驚くことに50%にまで増える可能性がある。クラウスが言うように、「人間が出す音が*耳をつんざくようになりつつあるのと同時に、大きな沈黙が自然界全体に広がりつつある」。

*「耳をつんざく」は、耳を突き破るほど大きな音がとどろくさま。

語彙リスト

unique	形	独自の
capture	動	とらえる
unrecognizable	形	認識できない
humankind	名	人類
impression	名	痕跡
highly	副	非常に
contain	動	含んでいる
estimate	動	推測する
species	名	種
extinction	名	絶滅
one-quarter	名	4分の1
astonishing	形	驚くべき
as S put it	熟	Sが言うように
at the same time that ~	熟	～と同時に
deafening	形	耳をつんざくような

▸単語10回CHECK 1 2 3 4 5 6 7 8 9 10

A Climate change is greatly affecting our world. It is contributing to an increase in extreme weather, more competition for resources such as water, and a greater number of disease-carrying insects, while at the same time having a negative effect on a wide variety of animals. These animals range from sea turtles to pandas to polar bears. Struggling to survive as Arctic ice melts due to global warming, the polar bear in particular has become a powerful symbol of the impact of climate change. However, there is another, often ignored indicator of the health of our planet: its soundscape.

B Soundscape ecology is the study of nature's sounds. Using a microphone and a recorder, American soundscape ecologist Bernie Krause has been recording the sounds of California's forests for many years: the gurgle of rivers and the melody of birdsong, the humming of insects. In the nearly 50 years Krause has been doing this, he has created a valuable resource for other ecologists to study. He believes strongly in the importance of recording soundscapes, saying, "Natural soundscapes give us information necessary to our understanding of the natural world. They allow us to perceive whether or not an environment is healthy."

C Krause's early recordings in the California forests were rich and full of life, a celebration of biodiversity. But when he returned last spring to his usual recording spot in Sugarloaf Ridge Stat. Park, what he heard was shocking. "The sounds of the forest had changed significantly," Krause says. "It was the first spring in my 77 years that I heard no birdsong at all." This was not entirely unexpected, he explains. California's forests have been severely affected by years of drought, or lack of rain, due to climate change. As the once-healthy forest habitat is damaged, the animals that live there are falling silent.

D Sadly, Krause has found similar changes in the soundscape of natural habitats around the world from the Amazon to Zimbabwe to Borneo. The growing silence of these soundscapes is an urgent warning about the effects of climate change. Krause says the changing soundscapes "speak strongly to all the climate issues we are now facing, from global warming to shifts in the number and variety of bird, frog and mammal populations." More than 50 percent of the thousands of unique habitats captured in his recordings are now almost completely silent, unrecognizable because of the damage that humankind has done to the environment.

E Krause says of his earlier recordings, "These are soundscapes that no one will hear again in their natural state. They exist today only as a kind of memory, a digital impression of what once existed." It is highly likely that Krause's recordings contain sounds made by undiscovered animals that have now disappeared and will never be known to us. Scientists estimate that in the next 25-30 years, up to one-quarter of the world's species may disappear, driven to extinction by climate change. That number could rise to an astonishing 50 percent by 2100. As Krause puts it, "A great silence is spreading over the natural world, at the same time that the sound of humankind is becoming deafening."

▸音読10回CHECK 1 2 3 4 5 6 7 8 9 10

BACKGROUND KNOWLEDGE

Soundscape

*soundscape*とは、landscape「風景」のlandをsoundに置き換えた言葉です。*sound*「**音**」＋*scape*「**風景**」で、「**音風景**」と訳されます。**風景には音が欠かせない**という考えから、音を環境の中で風景としてとらえる、ということです。

例えば、自然の風景を描写すると、そこには**鳥のさえずりが聞こえてくる景色**、**川のせせらぎが聞こえてくる景色**、**風で木々が揺れる景色**などさまざまです。**野生動物の生息地では、その鳴き声が聞こえてくる景色**もあります。

一方、**都市部では人の行き交う足音や電車の発車音が聞こえてくる景色**、**海岸部であれば波の音や船の汽笛の音**が聞こえてくる景色もあります。

近代では、**音を環境から切り離し、あまりにも客観的に扱ってきた**ため、もう一度**音を風景とセットの構図**でとらえ、そのうえで音を巡っての関係性に注目しようとする試みが*soundscape*です。

本問では、*soundscape***を気候変動に応用する試み**が紹介されていますが、もう1つの応用例として、**サウンドスケープデザイン**が挙げられます。例えば、人工的に庭を作る作業の造園に、**サウンドスケープデザイン**を応用します。

多少広めの庭に、**数本の木々を植える**のなら、**夏のセミの鳴き声や木々に集まる野鳥の鳴き声**があると、より自然に近い風景になるでしょう。

さらに、**庭に池を設置**するのなら、**カエルの鳴き声**、あるいは**鯉が泳ぐことで波打つ水の音**などがあると、より自然に近い庭園になるでしょう。

問題 10

社 会

孤独問題

別冊p.46／制限時間25分／582 words

解答

(問1) ア 4　イ 1　ウ 3　(問2) loneliness
(問3) 2　(問4) A 4　B 2　C 4

解説

(問1)

ア 孤独であることを選ぶ人はほとんどいない
1. 騒がしい隣人を排除することは難しい
2. 一緒に近くで暮らさざるを得ない人がたくさんいる
3. 孤独がどこから生まれるのかがわかる人は誰もいない
4. 孤独を好む人は多くはない

下線部(ア) **few choose to be lonely**は、p.125 語彙 POINT ❻ で学んだように、**fewが準否定語**で「**ほとんど〜ない**」と**数を打ち消す単語**とわかれば、「**孤独であることを選ぶ人はほとんどいない**」の意味とわかる。よって、**4. there are not many who prefer loneliness**が正解とわかる。

イ 人が目的意識や何かに貢献している実感をなくしたとき
1. 人が自分や他人のために何をすべきかがわからないとき
2. 社会が自然災害で混乱しているとき
3. 人々の中で政府への深い不信感があるとき
4. あなたが自分自身の将来を想像するようになるとき

下線部(イ)の**a sense of purpose and contribution**「**目的意識や何かに貢献している実感**」が、1で**what to do for oneself or for others**「**自分や他人のために何をすべきか**」にパラフレーズされているので、**1. when one does not know what to do for oneself or for others**が正解。**do for oneself**が**purpose**と、**do for others**が**contribution**と同義。

ウ 複数の世話をする責任
1. 高齢の患者に延命治療すべきかどうかを決める責任
2. 家事を担当するだけではなく、生計を立てる責任
3. 同時に2人以上の面倒を見る責任
4. 地域住民のさまざまな状況を考慮する責任

下線部(ウ) **multiple caring responsibilities**は、**家族が50年前と同じ機能を果たせない原因の具体例**として挙げられているので、**例えば自分の親の介護と、自分の子供の育児を1人でするような、いわゆるダブルケアという状況を指す**ことがわかる。よって、**3. responsibilities to look after more than one person at the same time**が正解。**caring「世話(介護)をする」**より、2は不適。

(問2)

下線部(エ) **one of the greatest social problems of our time「私たちの時代の最も大きな社会問題の1つ」**とは、**第2段落第2文**で初登場して、それ以降も何度も登場する**loneliness**が正解。

(問3)

(オ) 人が同じコミュニティにいる人の福祉にもっと関心を持てるような文化的変化が必要だ

↓

( ) 文化的変化が必要だ

1. さらに裕福な社会で、人々がお互いからもっと自立して暮らすことを可能にする
2. 人々に隣人の健康や安全、そして幸福をもっと考えるように促す
3. 病人や高齢者を支援するのに、人がより多くのお金を集めさせる
4. 人々に、昔の礼儀正しさや勤勉さの重要性を思い出させる

下線部(オ) **there needs to be a cultural shift so that people are more concerned about the welfare of those in their communities**のso that以下を言い換えるとどうなるかという問題。**so that S 助動詞**で「**Sが〜するように**」という意味なので、「**人が同じコミュニティにいる人の幸福をもっと気にかけるように**」の意味とわかる。下線部(オ)の**be concerned about「〜を気にかける」**が、2の**think more about**にパラフレーズされていることに気付けば、2が正解とわかる。

不正解の選択肢を見ていくと、1はmore independently「もっと自立して」が誤り。3のraise more money「もっとお金を集める」のような表現はないし、4のthe politeness and diligence of the old days「昔の礼儀正しさや勤勉さ」のような記述もないので不適。

(問4)

A 1. 人口の高齢化が原因で、自立して生きていける十分な技術を持った世代が生まれた。
2. 一人で暮らす人の数が、都市部では増えているが、郊外の地域では増えていない。
3. メンタルヘルス財団の報告によると、若者の孤独が原因で、人の交流の仕方に変化が生じている。
4. ジョン・ダンが言いたいのは、私たちの誰も世界から完全に孤立しては生きていけないということだ。

4は、**第1段落第1文No man is an island, entire of itself; every man is a piece of the continent, a part of the main**「**人間は、誰もそれだけで自足している島ではない。いかなる人も大陸の一片であり、大海原の一部なのだ**」に一致する。

不正解の選択肢を見ていくと、1は本文に記述なし。2は、前半部分が**第2段落第4文後半the rise of the solo dweller**「**一人暮らしの増加**」**に一致**するが、**後半部分in the city, but not in the suburban areasが本文に記述なし**。3は、**第2段落第4文後半social changes such as the rise of the solo dweller, combined with an aging population**, are changing the way people interact with each otherに不一致。あくまで**一人暮らしの増加や人口の高齢化のような社会の変化が原因**で、3のような**若者の孤独が原因という記述は本文になし。**

B 1. ミッチェルは、パムを死別が引き起こす孤独を乗り越える人の、よい例だと考えている。
2. パムは、夫が4年前に亡くなる以前と同じ世界観を抱くことはできない。
3. パムは将来の夫を熱心に探しているが、とても多くの候補がいるので、1人だけには絞り切れない。
4. パムは夫の面倒を見ることにうんざりしており、いつか彼が自分自身の面倒を見られるようになることを望んでいる。

2は**第4段落第1文 losing your husband or wife can have a really detrimental impact on how people feel about the world「夫や妻を失うことは、人が世の中をどう感じるかに、本当に有害な影響を与える可能性がある」**、**同段落第2文It is a feeling that Pam, whose husband died four years ago, identifies with.「それは、4年前に夫を亡くしたパムが自分を重ね合わせる感情だ」**に一致。それ以外の選択肢は本文に記述なし。

C 1. マカロックによると、現代の人は、50年前よりも、家族に対して愛着が少ない。
2. マカロックは、さまざまな営利事業を推進するのに、私たちはもっと多くの投資を必要としていると主張する。
3. マカロックは、隣人に挨拶(あいさつ)するような些細な行為は、現代社会では意味があるとは思っていない。
4. マカロックは、人がもっと親密になれるように、現代の社会ネットワークを革新することが重要だと主張する。

4は、**第7段落第3文 But he says there needs to be a cultural shift so that people are more concerned about the welfare of those in their communities.「しかし、人が同じコミュニティにいる人の福祉により関心を持てるような文化的変化が必要だと彼(マカロック)は言う」**に一致。本文の**a cultural shift so that people are more concerned about the welfare of those in their communities**が、4の**innovating today's social networks so that people can get closer**にパラフレーズされていることに注意する。

不正解の選択肢を見ていくと、1は**第5段落最終文It's not because they are bad or uncaring families「それ(50年前と家族の機能が変わっていること)は、家族が悪いとか思いやりのない家族だということではない」**と不一致。2は、**第6段落第2文**にミッチェルの発言で「**多くの投資が必要だ**」とあるが、**social help「社会的支援」**に対してであって、**commercial enterprises「営利事業」**とは書かれていないので不適。

3は、**第7段落最終文 "Just a basic level of social behavior, such as saying hello, or asking if people are OK, can have an impact," he says.「『挨拶をする、あるいは大丈夫かどうか尋ねるような、ごく基本的なレベルの社会的行為が影響力を持つことがある』と彼(マカロック)は言う」**に反するので不適。**doubt that**で、**don't think that「~と思わない」**と同義表現であることに注意する。

構文図解

"No man is an island, entire of itself; every man is a piece of the continent, a part of the main," wrote the poet John Donne [in the 17th Century].

O 同格のカンマ 同格のカンマ 「大海原」(古英語) V S M

Some people seek isolation, but few choose 〈to be lonely〉. Loneliness not only makes us unhappy, but it is bad [for us]. It can lead to a lack (of confidence and mental health problems like depression, stress and anxiety). A report (by the Mental Health Foundation) suggests 〈loneliness among young people is increasing〉; [at the same time], social changes (such as the rise of the solo dweller), [combined with an aging population], are changing the way (people interact with each other).

S V O S V O (不定詞 名詞的用法) S M V O C (loneliness) S V C M (loneliness) S V O M 前置詞のlike depression, stress, anxietyの3つの接続 S M V 名詞節のthatの省略 O M S M 分詞構文 M V O the way SV M

So is modern life making us lonely? People feel lonely for different reasons, says Michelle Mitchell, charity director general of Age UK, but it tends to be triggered [by a big life event]. "It can be poor health, illness, money, children moving away, feeling cut off from family or community, a lack of access to transport, redundancy or career problems or divorce. Often it's 〈when people lose a sense of purpose and contribution〉."

V S V O C O 孤独を指す V S 同格のカンマ S′ S V M (a big life eventを指す) S V C (a big life eventを指す) M S V 「〜するとき」 C

"Bereavement is also a big issue — losing your husband or wife can have a really detrimental impact on how people feel about the world," Mitchell says.

O 動名詞 「どのように〜か」 S V

本文訳

「人間は、誰もそれだけで自足している島ではない。いかなる人も、大陸の一片であり、大海原(おおうなばら)の一部なのだ」と17世紀にジョン・ダンという詩人が書いた。

孤立を求める人はいるが、孤独を選ぶ人はほとんどいない。孤独は私たちを不幸にするだけでなく、健康にも悪いものだ。それは、自信喪失や鬱(うつ)、ストレス、不安のような精神衛生の問題を引き起こすことがある。メンタルヘルス財団の報告によると、若者の孤独が増加しているとわかっている。同時に、高齢化とあわせて、一人暮らしの増加のような社会の変化が、人が交流する方法を変えつつある。

すると、現代の生活のせいで、私たちは孤独になるのか？ 人はさまざまな理由で孤独を感じると、*エイジUKの会長であるミシェル・ミッチェルは言うが、それは大きなライフイベントで引き起こされる傾向にある。「それは健康の悪化、病気、お金、子供との別居、家族やコミュニティからの隔絶、移動手段の欠如、リストラ、キャリアの問題や離婚といったことである。それはたいてい、人が目的意識や何かに貢献している実感をなくしたときだ」。

「死別も大きな問題だ。夫や妻を失うことは、人が世の中をどう感じるかに、本当に有害な影響を与える可能性がある」とミッチェルは言う。

*「エイジUK」は、イギリスに住む50歳以上の人が、安心して快適な生活を送れるように支援する団体。

語彙リスト

単語	意味
island	名 島
entire	名 全体
a piece of	熟 ～の一片
continent	名 大陸
poet	名 詩人
seek	動 求める
isolation	名 孤立
lonely	形 孤独な
lead to	熟 引き起こす
confidence	名 自信
mental	形 精神的な
depression	名 鬱(うつ)
anxiety	名 不安
solo	形 単独の
dweller	名 住人
combine A with B	熟 AをBと結び付ける
aging	形 高齢の
interact with	熟 ～と交流する
charity	名 慈善事業
director general	名 会長
trigger	動 引き起こす
cut off	熟 切り離す
redundancy	名 解雇
divorce	名 離婚
contribution	名 貢献
bereavement	名 死別
have an impact on	熟 ～に影響を与える
detrimental	形 有害な

▸単語10回CHECK 1 2 3 4 5 6 7 8 9 10

構文図解

It is a feeling (that Pam, whose husband died four years ago, identifies with). "You meet other men, who are on their own. That's not what I am looking for. What am I looking for? I'm looking for my husband, aren't I, and I'm never going to find him," she says.

bereavementを指す / S V C / 関係代名詞のthat / M / O / 通常の男女の出会い / 関係代名詞 / am notの短縮形がないのでaren'tで代用した表現 / S V

But [while bereavement may be inevitable], there's a sense (modern society is exacerbating other triggers of loneliness). Dr. Andrew McCulloch, chief executive of the Mental Health Foundation, argues 〈that although there is no hard historic data to show loneliness — which is arguably subjective — getting worse, there is some sociological evidence〉. "We have data (that suggests people's social networks have got smaller and families are not providing the same level of social context they may have done 50 years ago). It's not because they are bad or uncaring families, but it's to do with geographical distance, marriage breakdown, multiple caring responsibilities and longer working hours," he says.

M M V S / 関係詞の省略 / M / S / 同格のカンマ / M / V / 名詞節のthat / O / 不定詞 形容詞的用法 / show O doingのdoing / 名詞節のthatの省略 / S V O / 関係代名詞のthat / M / 家族が50年前と同程度の社会的機能を果たしていないこと / 関係詞の省略 / familiesを指す / O / 現代の家族を指す / 家族が50年前と同程度の社会的機能を果たしていないこと / geographical distanceからlonger working hoursまでの4つの接続 / S V

But [if modern society is making us lonelier], what can be done [to counter it]?

不定詞 副詞的用法 / M S V / M / lonelinessを指す

本文訳

それは、4年前に夫を亡くしたパムが自分を重ね合わせる感情だ。「あなたたちは結婚していない別の男性と出会うわね。でもそれは私が探していることではないの。私は何を探しているのかって？ 私が探しているのは夫でしょ？ でも私は決して彼を見つけることはできないの」と彼女は言う。

しかし、死別は避けられないかもしれないが、現代社会が孤独の他の要因を悪化させている感がある。おそらく主観的なもので、孤独が悪化していることを示す確かな史実に基づくデータはないけれども、一定の社会学的な証拠はあると、メンタルヘルス財団の最高責任者であるアンドリュー・マカロック博士は主張する。「人を結ぶ社会的なつながりが小さくなり、家族が50年前にもたらしていたのと、同程度の社会的機能を果たしていないことを示すデータがある。それは、その家族が悪いとか思いやりのない家族だからではなくて、地理的な距離、結婚生活の崩壊、複数の世話をする責任、長時間労働に関係するものだ」と彼は言う。

しかし、もし現代社会が私たちをより孤独にさせるなら、それに対抗するために、何ができるのか？

語彙リスト

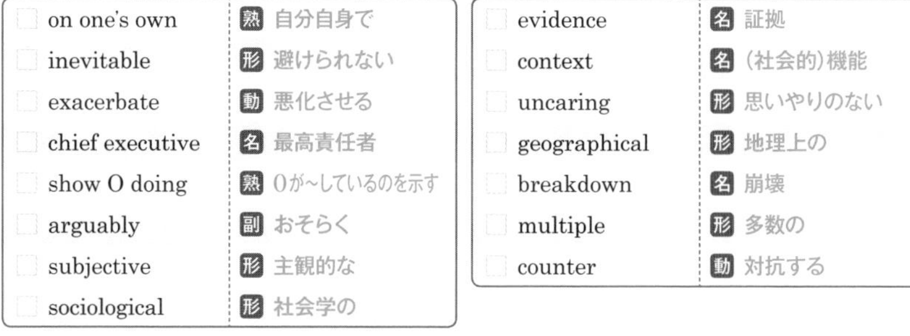

on one's own	熟	自分自身で
inevitable	形	避けられない
exacerbate	動	悪化させる
chief executive	名	最高責任者
show O doing	熟	Oが~しているのを示す
arguably	副	おそらく
subjective	形	主観的な
sociological	形	社会学の
evidence	名	証拠
context	名	(社会的)機能
uncaring	形	思いやりのない
geographical	形	地理上の
breakdown	名	崩壊
multiple	形	多数の
counter	動	対抗する

▸単語10回CHECK 1 2 3 4 5 6 7 8 9 10

構文図解

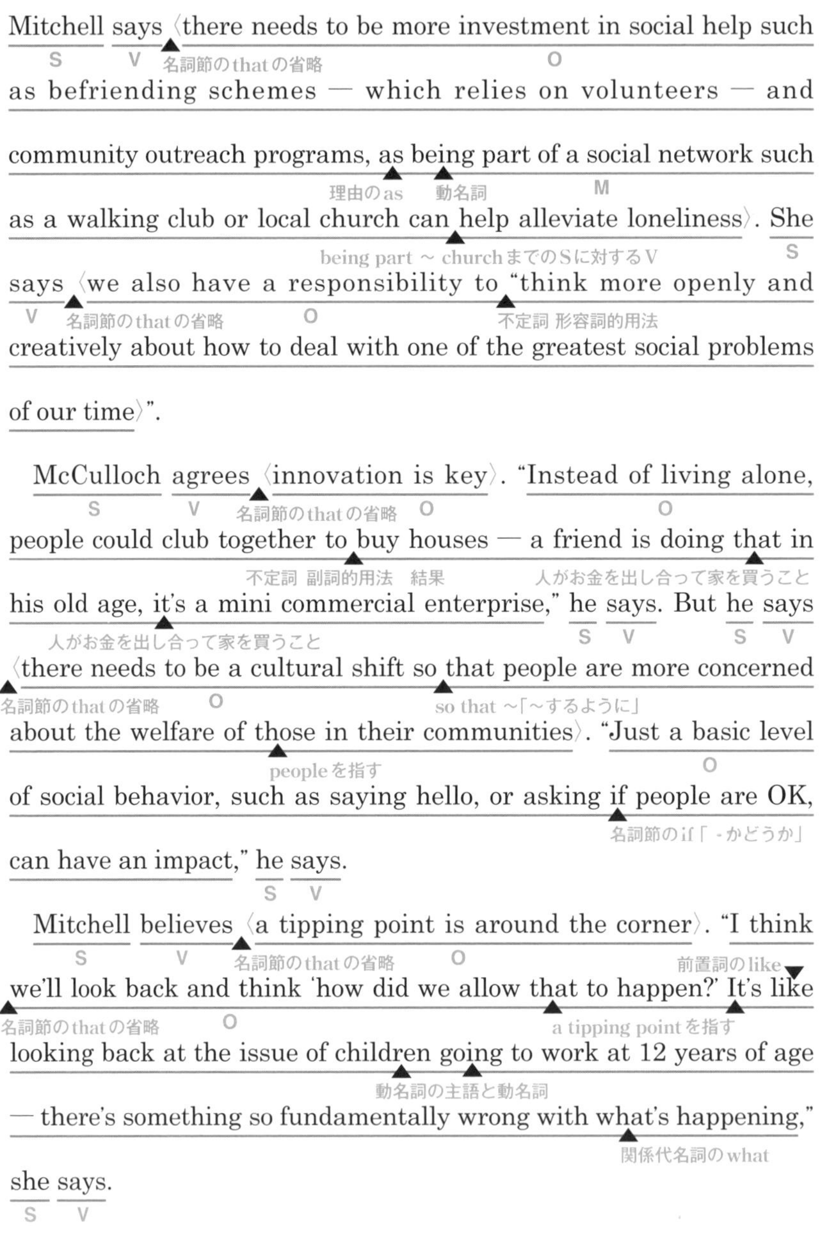

Mitchell says 〈there needs to be more investment in social help such as befriending schemes — which relies on volunteers — and community outreach programs, as being part of a social network such as a walking club or local church can help alleviate loneliness〉. She says 〈we also have a responsibility to "think more openly and creatively about how to deal with one of the greatest social problems of our time〉".

McCulloch agrees 〈innovation is key〉. "Instead of living alone, people could club together to buy houses — a friend is doing that in his old age, it's a mini commercial enterprise," he says. But he says 〈there needs to be a cultural shift so that people are more concerned about the welfare of those in their communities〉. "Just a basic level of social behavior, such as saying hello, or asking if people are OK, can have an impact," he says.

Mitchell believes 〈a tipping point is around the corner〉. "I think we'll look back and think 'how did we allow that to happen?' It's like looking back at the issue of children going to work at 12 years of age — there's something so fundamentally wrong with what's happening," she says.

本文訳

ウォーキングクラブや地域の教会のような社会的なつながりの一員になることで孤独が和らぐ手助けとなるので、ボランティアに頼っている友達作り計画や地域の福祉を広めるための企画といった社会的支援に、もっと投資する必要があると、ミッチェルは言う。私たちも「今の時代の最も大きな社会問題の1つに対処する方法を、もっとオープンに創造的に考える」責任があると彼女は言う。

マカロックは、*イノベーションが重要だと賛同する。「一人で生活する代わりに、人がお金を出し合って家を購入することもできる。ある友人は高齢になってそうしており、それは小さな営利事業にあたる」と彼は言う。しかし、人が同じコミュニティにいる人の福祉にもっと関心を持てるような文化的変化が必要だと彼は言う。「挨拶をする、あるいは大丈夫かどうか尋ねるような、ごく基本的なレベルの社会的行為が影響力を持つことがある」と彼は言う。

ミッチェルは、転換点がもうすぐだと信じている。「私たちは振り返り、『どうやってそんなことが起きるのを許容していたのか』と考えるだろうと思う。それは、子供たちが12歳で働きに出た問題を振り返るようなものだ、今起きていることには根本的に間違っていることがある」と彼女は言う。

*「イノベーション」は「革新」の意味で、新しい技術や制度で変革を起こすこと。

語彙リスト

investment	名 投資	club together	熟 (金を)出し合う
befriend	動 友達になる	enterprise	名 事業
scheme	名 計画	shift	名 変化
rely on	熟 ～に頼る	be concerned about	熟 ～に関心を持つ
outreach program	名 奉仕活動計画	welfare	名 福祉
alleviate	動 緩和する	tipping point	名 大きな転換点
openly	副 公然と	around the corner	熟 すぐそばに
innovation	名 革新	look back at	熟 ～を振り返る
key	名 重要なこと	fundamentally	副 根本的に

▸単語10回CHECK 1 2 3 4 5 6 7 8 9 10

“No man is an island, entire of itself; every man is a piece of the continent, a part of the main,” wrote the poet John Donne in the 17th Century.

Some people seek isolation, but few choose to be lonely. Loneliness not only makes us unhappy, but it is bad for us. It can lead to a lack of confidence and mental health problems like depression, stress and anxiety. A report by the Mental Health Foundation suggests loneliness among young people is increasing; at the same time, social changes such as the rise of the solo dweller, combined with an aging population, are changing the way people interact with each other.

So is modern life making us lonely? People feel lonely for different reasons, says Michelle Mitchell, charity director general of Age UK, but it tends to be triggered by a big life event. “It can be poor health, illness, money, children moving away, feeling cut off from family or community, a lack of access to transport, redundancy or career problems or divorce. Often it's when people lose a sense of purpose and contribution.”

“Bereavement is also a big issue — losing your husband or wife can have a really detrimental impact on how people feel about the world,” Mitchell says. It is a feeling that Pam, whose husband died four years ago, identifies with. “You meet other men, who are on their own. That's not what I am looking for. What am I looking for? I'm looking for my husband, aren't I, and I'm never going to find him,” she says.

But while bereavement may be inevitable, there's a sense modern society is exacerbating other triggers of loneliness. Dr. Andrew McCulloch, chief executive of the Mental Health Foundation, argues that although there is no hard historic data to show loneliness — which is arguably subjective — getting worse, there is some sociological evidence. “We have data that suggests people's social networks have got smaller and families are not providing the same level of social context they may have done 50 years ago. It's not because they are bad or uncaring families, but it's to do with geographical distance, marriage breakdown, multiple caring responsibilities and longer working hours," he says.

But if modern society is making us lonelier, what can be done to counter it? Mitchell says there needs to be more investment in social help such as befriending schemes — which relies on volunteers — and community outreach programs, as being part of a social network such as a walking club or local church can help alleviate loneliness. She says we also have a responsibility to "think more openly and creatively about how to deal with one of the greatest social problems of our time".

McCulloch agrees innovation is key. "Instead of living alone, people could club together to buy houses — a friend is doing that in his old age, it's a mini commercial enterprise," he says. But he says there needs to be a cultural shift so that people are more concerned about the welfare of those in their communities. "Just a basic level of social behavior, such as saying hello, or asking if people are OK, can have an impact," he says.

Mitchell believes a tipping point is around the corner. "I think we'll look back and think 'how did we allow that to happen?' It's like looking back at the issue of children going to work at 12 years of age — there's something so fundamentally wrong with what's happening," she says.

▸音読10回CHECK 1 2 3 4 5 6 7 8 9 10

BACKGROUND KNOWLEDGE

孤独は1日15本のタバコに匹敵する

孤独問題については、前作の『**大学入試　レベル別英語長文問題　ソリューション3 トップレベル**』の問題4のコラムで触れました。本問にもある**孤独問題は**、現在**世界的に蔓延（まんえん）している深刻な問題**です。

ニュースサイト「ビジネス・インサイダー」オーストラリア版では、例えば、**満足な社会的支援を受けていない孤立状態にあると、その被害はタバコを1日15本吸うのと同程度だ**と発表されました。**孤独を感じることにより、そのストレスから体の中で炎症が発生**し、**血管系の疾患を発症する**という研究もあります。

米ブリガムヤング大学教授（心理学）のジュリアン・ホルトランスタッド氏は、先行する研究のデータを集めて分析し、**孤独感を引き起こす社会的つながりの少なさは、喫煙、飲酒、運動不足、肥満よりも大きい短命リスク**だと指摘しました。

そして、“**孤独感は友人の友人の友人まで伝染する**”と、孤独研究の第一人者でシカゴ大学教授の故ジョン・カシオッポ氏は言います。**元々友人が少なくて孤独感を抱いている人ほど人間に対する不信感が強く、数少ない友人との関係も断ち切ってしまう**ようです。関係を絶たれた**その友人も孤独感にさいなまれ、同じことを繰り返して、負の連鎖が起こりやすい**そうです。

学力、体力、経済力など、大切な力はたくさんありますが、孤立を避けるために“**人と上手く付き合っていく力**”、“**協調性**”が、ますます大切になってくる時代なのかもしれません。

おわりに

本書を最後まで読んでくださった読者の方一人一人に、心より御礼申し上げます。本書は、この本の前身となる『**大学入試　レベル別英語長文問題ソリューション**』の**音読がしやすい短めの語数の長文を揃えるという特長を維持**しつつ、さらに**扱うテーマを最新のものに厳選**することで、**志望校の過去問演習に入る直前の1冊**をイメージして執筆しました。

試験本番の1週間前でも終われるように、問題数をあえて10題に限定しています。

問題を解いて**解説を読んで終わりの長文の勉強は、もう終わり**にしましょう。重要なのは、**1つの長文を自分のものにして先に進むこと、出てきた単語を必ず覚えて、10回音読すること**です。必要なのは、**皆さんの能動的な姿勢**です。

本書はまだハイレベルという中程度のレベルなので、本書の10題の英文を完璧にしたら、ぜひ次のトップレベルへと進んでください。トップレベルにおいても、**音読に最適な最新テーマの良問を10題**揃えています。本シリーズが、あなたの人生を変えるシリーズとなることを願っています。

最後に、本書の企画・編集を担当してくださった（株）かんき出版の前澤美恵子様、本書に素敵なデザインを施してくださったワーク・ワンダースの鈴木智則様、本書の校正を念入りにしてくださった（株）オルタナプロの渋谷超様やその他の先生方、『ソリューション最新テーマ編』シリーズのアイディアを授けてくださった（株）A.ver教務部長の中森泰樹先生、最後までお付き合いいただいた読者の皆様に、心から御礼申しあげます。

肘井　学

【著者紹介】

肘井　学（ひじい・がく）

◉——慶應義塾大学文学部英米文学専攻卒業。全国のさまざまな予備校をへて、リクルートが主催するネット講義サービス「スタディサプリ」で教鞭をとり、高校生、受験生から英語を学びなおす社会人まで、圧倒的な満足度を誇る。

◉——「スタディサプリ」で公開される「英文読解」の講座は、年間25万人の生徒が受講する超人気講座となっている。さらに「東大英語」「京大英語」を担当し、受講者に多くの成功体験を与えている。

◉——週刊英和新聞「朝日ウィークリー（Asahi Weekly）」にてコラムを連載するなど、幅広く活躍中。

◉——著書に『大学入試 肘井学の読解のための英文法が面白いほどわかる本』『大学入試 肘井学の ゼロから英語長文が面白いほどわかる本』『大学入試 ゼロから英文法が面白いほどわかる本』『大学入試 肘井学の 作文のための英文法が面白いほどわかる本』（KADOKAWA）、『大学入試 すぐわかる英文法』『大学入試 すぐ書ける自由英作文』『大学入試 絶対できる英語リスニング』（教学社）、『高校の英文法が１冊でしっかりわかる本』『高校の英文読解が１冊でしっかりわかる本』（かんき出版）などがある。

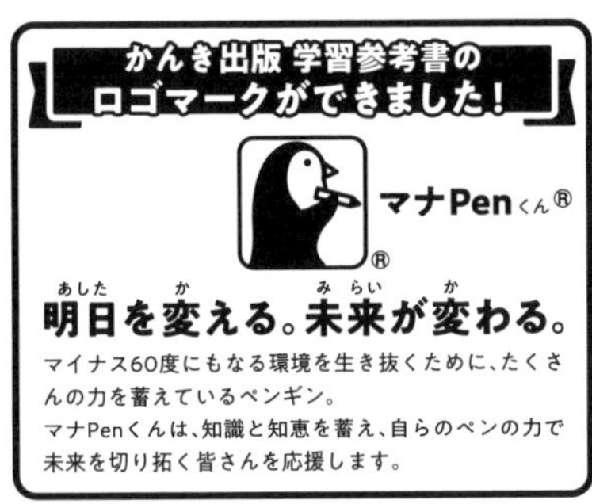

大学入試 レベル別英語長文問題ソリューション最新テーマ編２　ハイレベル

2021年11月18日　第１刷発行
2024年11月14日　第５刷発行

著　者——肘井　学
発行者——齊藤　龍男
発行所——株式会社かんき出版
東京都千代田区麹町4-1-4 西脇ビル　〒102-0083
電話　営業部：03(3262)8011㈹　編集部：03(3262)8012㈹
FAX　03(3234)4421　振替　00100-2-62304
https://kanki-pub.co.jp/

印刷所——大日本印刷株式会社

　ISBN978-4-7612-3050-0 C7382